DATE DUE

TRADITION AND ECONOMY
IN VILLAGE INDIA

INTERNATIONAL LIBRARY OF SOCIOLOGY
AND SOCIAL RECONSTRUCTION

Founded by Karl Mannheim

Editor: W. J. H. Sprott

A catalogue of the books available in the INTERNATIONAL LIBRARY OF SOCIOLOGY AND SOCIAL RECONSTRUCTION, and new books in preparation for the Library will be found at the end of this volume.

TRADITION AND ECONOMY
IN VILLAGE INDIA

by

K. Ishwaran

Foreword by
Conrad Arensberg

LONDON
ROUTLEDGE & KEGAN PAUL
NEW YORK: THE HUMANITIES PRESS

*First published in 1966
by Routledge & Kegan Paul Ltd
Broadway House, 68–74 Carter Lane
London, E.C.4*

*Printed in Great Britain
by C. Tinling & Co. Ltd
Liverpool, London and Prescot*

CONTENTS

To
Nels Anderson

FOREWORD

THE EFFICACY OF modern village or community studies
lies in their deriving better understandings of the structure
and function of institutions. They perform this office of
social science by analysing the living workings of institutions in the experience of human beings struggling between
traditional values and modern imperatives of change. A
study of an institution *in vivo* shows its connections with
others and its functions for the social and cultural system
of a civilisation as these have evolved in the local and
national pasts. Such a study shows no less the self-righting
of such systems under the blows of novelty and the lures of
the outside world, and thus the adaptation of society and
culture to such change. Thus the book before us is a community study, in that it lays bare before us a living village,
in an interesting and too little reported region of the great
and complex land of India. It is also, most importantly, the
study of a local variant of a traditional economic institution,
called elsewhere the *Jajmani* system, better the traditional
economy of clientage and patronage, uniting service castes
in ritual and craft services to the landowners and cultivators
of a corporate village, an object of interest and speculation
for social science since its discovery in the seminal historical
studies of Sir Henry Maine. But it is most certainly, also,
the study of such an institution not only in its setting but
also as well in its present role: that of supporting Indian
villagers through the travails (and the rewards) of national
incorporation and economic revolution. In this, as is the
virtue of good community studies and good social science
analysis, the study of a purely local scene bears not only
upon our current understanding of a nation and a civilisation, but also upon our world-wide concern with a major

vii

Foreword

tide of our age: what Redfield[1] called the transformation of peasantry and others more pedestrian entitle the urbanisation of the world.

In good modern world-wide company as it is, this book joins a still more select though ever-growing few. It is done by an Indian national, out of concern for his own land and addressed in part to his fellow nationals. He joins thus a long and honourable tradition of anthropology and sociology marked by earlier names such as Anantha Krishna Iyer and Sarat Chandra Roy and brilliantly continued by those of M. N. Srinivas and S. C. Dube today, to name only a few of the many modern Indians contributing to scholarship of importance at once practical and significant both at home and abroad. It is unique, indeed, in that the author, returning to his natal region, does so with the distinction of having already written, as the first to do so, a prior book of well wrought sociological analysis[2] by a non-European upon a European scene, thus turning the tables on the many Westerners who have delved for sociological comparisons, not all with the same grace and the same success, in Indian and other non-Western communities.

Professor Ishwaran thus presents us with his sample of Indian civilisation and Kanarese (Mysorean) culture in a single, still vital and viable village. He well attests to its representativeness, not with numbers and statistical proportions, but rather with ethnographically valid identification, description, and elucidation of its still binding values and rules of behaviour, its still continuing social organisation, its still living religious *ethos*. He shows us how these strands of tradition, these things of the Indian spirit, so well known from literature, piety, and art as well as history, still animate the villagers at home and among themselves, even in a world modernising this village to the extent of

[1] Redfield, Robert. *Peasant Society and Culture: An Anthropological Approach to Civilisation.* Chicago: University of Chicago Press, 1956.
[2] Ishwaran, K. *Family Life in the Netherlands.* Van Keulen. The Hague, 1959.

its imminent engulfment in a nearby industrialising urban administrative centre and in a nation making good its political integration of the region even to the extent of establishing over the continuing traditional village caste, street, and lineage councils a new local government (the new statutory *panchayat*) and local elections (in 1957 the villagers for the first time electing a minority Maratha rather than a landed, dominant-caste Lingayat to its chairmanship). In showing these things Professor Ishwaran writes with a sureness about their inner force and a sympathetic feeling for their symmetry as aspects of a way of life that only an Indian could impart to the record.

As an Indian national, too, Professor Ishwaran is concerned not only in showing the colour and emotion of the realities of his village and its country but also in demonstrating to fellow citizens and national planners and administrators, as well as to fellow social scientists everywhere, the present seemingly quite healthy local merger of traditional ways and values with acceptances of the outside and modernising forces of nation-building and world commerce effected by his village subjects. He is concerned with a gap of understanding, perhaps even a failure of empathy. Administrators and planners, intent on modernising and face-to-face with intractable social problems demanding remedial and organising action, may perhaps underestimate their need to understand the countryside and its people and underestimate, or dismiss as resistances, the values and the structure of the society they seek to move to change. Social scientists, too, perhaps fail to put their findings about the continuities, the antiquities, and the local persistences of culture and social organisation in which they immerse themselves and about which they write with such fervent academic enthusiasm into usable forms of information and advice. Professor Ishwaran seeks, I believe successfully, to offer his finding, that the coexistence of change and continuity can carry a balance between internal stability in old ways and external adjustment to new ones which gives the village its distinctive present character and viability, in terms aimed to bridge that gap. He aims to provide common ground for the social scientist and the administrator and to give them both a better grasp of the reality of the villager's situation and of his commitment in it. When he demonstrates, to quote his own words, that his people 'while accepting the new . . . never gives up the old outright,' he seems to be saying this process of merger of new and old is exactly the one which can be expected to endure and for which plans should realistically be shaped.

Apart from this contribution to policy, the book offers also much new matter for science. It offers an illumination of a new region of India for sociology and a new exploration of a Kanarese and even a Lingayat variant of familiar but complex institutions and social structure. Here the book adds significantly to the roster of comparable studies of modern Indian villages and sharpens our understanding of the universalities shared by them in highlighting the variant particularities proper to each region.

Professor Ishwaran is at his best in his analysis of the traditional social structure, its principles of organisation, and its supports in religious concensus. It is of course the more remarkable that here the Brahman and the Kshatriya play so little role. Reformist as this region and its dominant sect have been, however old and pre-Aryan we can guess the ultimate origin of the values and structural principles of Indian society to have been, common elements of Indian civilisation in family structure, lineage, caste and sub-caste achieve here also not only a hierarchical ranking of persons, groups, occupations and services, places, and cults structured like those of other parts of India, with different names, but more significantly for students of comparaitve social structure, cultural integration, and economic systems, a very similar system of reciprocation and redistributive relationships uniting land-owning, employing yeomen and their service-caste and field-labour clients. Brahman and Kshatriya are not present, formally, but their roles have

reappeared and the web of their interconnections been retained among the sectarians and their Maratha, Muslim,
and other-caste fellow-villagers. The Lingayat sub-castes
have structured themselves, together with these others,
into such roles; and though they are still in many ways
solitary, united perhaps in their surprisingly Protestant or
Calvinist-Puritan-seeming sanctification of work and independence, as well, of course, as in their common ritual and
partial commensality, they remain in all this, however
Weberian their work ethos, as Indian as ever.

Hierarchy and balanced intergroup opposition are structural principles often appealed to today in modern social
anthropology to account for polycephalous and segmental,
rather than monolithic and monarchic or bureaucratic
central organisation. They are well demonstrated here once
again. They show once more the balanced oligarchic and
traditionally republican nature of the Indian village. The
village looks more and more like a residential and land-use
corporation of the dominant caste of a countryside, exoga-
mously bound over a circle of villages or surrounding region,
endogamously related as caste and village brothers in their
own *panchayats* of lineages, streets (here in the South), and
village, intricately bound to their clients of other castes,
themselves comparably organised in lineages, streets, and
marriage circles as well as in councils of their own. However much it loses religious and traditional services, relationships, and loyalties today and replaces them with
external economic and political ties, the traditional village,
caste, and patronage system offered and still seems to offer
a local and semiautonomous field of institutionalised social
control, operating of course always at a level below royal
and imperial (and now national) authority, expressed in
many and repeated open discussions and negotiations,
rooted in endless patience and permissiveness with deviance
and divergence of self-interest and sub-group concern.
Hierarchical as it may have been (or still be), the ranking of
persons it displayed was based not alone on power and

ownership of lands but upon performance in the values of
a common ethos of generosity and piety as well.

Thus hierarchy and balanced opposition of segments
in changing coalition are not enough, among structural
principles invoked in modern social anthropology, to explain the village and its social and ethical order. Professor
Ishwaran shows that in the *Aya* system (the patronal system
of his 'Shivapur') he describes and in the celebrations and
services of the religious calendar and of the *rites of passage*
of fellow villagers, in which all take part in their ranked
parts and degrees, another principle proves a far better key.
Hierarchy itself, we learn, is a resultant of the ordering of
changing positions in the endless repetitions in the village
of traditional givings, receivings, and repayings. Reciproci-
ties not only validate hierarchy, they make the system itself.

In this discovery Professor Ishwaran expands well some
of the hypotheses of other analysts of today and he is well
aware of the import for social theory of his conclusion. The
traditional patronal and reciprocal economic system of the
village is not reducible to modern economics or law or
politics, he says. These live by other values and are created
by events of relationship of other structuring than those of
gift-giving. The *Aya* system is 'a noteworthy institution
belonging to the family of gift systems of which there is a
wide variety scattered practically all over the world.'[3]
Identifying and understanding these institutions of the many
civilisations of the world, the author might well be saying,
and appraising and reconciling their continuing, not to be
lightly discarded differences from recent institutions of the
Western world, is a major task for social science and a step
in its progress towards usefulness that cannot be ignored
if a true world-wide modernity is to be achieved and if

[3] See Polayni, Karl, Conrad M. Arensberg and Harry W. Pearson.
Trade and Market in the Early Empires. Glencoe: Free Press, 1957.

For redistributive and reciprocal economic systems, and especially
the chapter by Walter C. Neale on 'Reciprocity and Redistribution in
The Indian Village: Sequel to Some Notable Discussions.'

Foreword

India and other now transforming countries of ancient tradition are to come to know themselves and their fates and to come to win through to a better self-guidance.

CONRAD A. ARENSBERG

Columbia University,
New York.
November, 1965.

ACKNOWLEDGEMENTS

THIS STUDY WAS made possible by a grant-in-aid from the Research Programme Committee of the Planning Commission, Government of India. It had to be carried out while I was also occupied with my teaching and administrative duties at Karnatak University, Dharwar, which is conveniently near Shivapur, the village studied. I feel obliged to the Research Programme Committee and to Dr. D. K. Malhotra, member-secretary of the Committee, who was generous in extending help.

This study extended from 1960 to 1964, and out of it will come two additional reports dealing with Shivapur. In the course of this field study I was enabled to carry on my obligations to my extended family, thanks largely to the help of my wife, Wobine, and I am happy here to express my gratitude to her. Her assistance was most helpful in completing this assignment.

I am indebted also to my friends and colleagues for help in preparing the manuscript. I am no less indebted to the authorities of the York University of Toronto, Canada, who generously provided secretarial assistance.

Finally, I must express my appreciation to the people of Shivapur. I will not easily forget their generosity, patience and friendliness.

K. ISHWARAN

York University,
Toronto, Canada.

PREFACE

THE PRESENT TREATISE owes its origin to a larger study of an Indian village society which has been in progress since the beginning of 1960. It focuses attention mainly on one aspect, the economic, but not as an isolated phenomenon. The fundamental framework of the total social context has not been lost sight of. The network of social relations concealed beneath a very simple-looking community is very complex, and the high degree of integration of these diverse elements into a common cultural system highly developed. The economy of the village has been the subject of much study in India, especially at the hands of foreign students. An impressive body of literature has gathered round the theme. This literature is, however, somewhat unsatisfactory for two reasons. Firstly, there is a tendency in it to look at the Indian village from a foreign viewpoint, which fails to enter into the spirit of the system. Secondly, there is no awareness that it is an integrated whole, and to reduce it to a mere economic system is to distort it. Moreover, it is not realised that this society has survived essentially on a traditional foundation which was at once economic, social, moral, political, legal, aesthetic and morphological.

The methodology here adopted contains three elements. Firstly, it involves observation of, and participation in, the life of the community under study. Secondly, it involves a comparative study of similar social systems elsewhere in the world. Thirdly, it also involves a linguistic approach in the sense that certain key words of the language of the community have been analysed to yield sociologically significant meaning. While the first led to the collection of an overwhelming wealth of empirical data, the second led to the seeking of similarity of patterns in comparable social backgrounds. The same basic pattern may operate in different social contexts. No true understanding of a society and its forms of life are possible without a correct understanding of key terms that dominate the language of the society. The approach is neither wholly inductive nor wholly deductive. On the one hand one has to begin with a certain operational, conceptual framework on a deductive basis, and, on the other hand, one has to test it in the light of the empirical data. The attempt has been made to keep scrupulously to the well-known rules of the scientific method.

The techniques employed were to be helpful in understanding the economic phenomena in the setting of the total social context. Participation in the local life and a feeling for its words, growing out of belonging to the same kind of broad cultural context, were of invaluable assistance. Studies such as this appear to be of special importance now that the Government of India, on its own and with the help of foreign agencies like the Ford Foundation, has taken upon itself the very difficult task of transforming the traditional peasant society in India through planned economic development. Such a task can hardly be fulfilled without intense studies of village society. This is just now the ideal time for an assessment of such a society since the change is still going on. Soon it may be too late. The Research Programme Committee of the Planning Commission was good enough to provide the necessary finances to conduct this study. The interest of the Planning Commission was to find out how best the village society could be changed. This was an applied, practical approach. But such a study is not possible without a preliminary theoretical framework. The Government of India may find this study useful to that end. Today there has grown up an unfortunate dichotomy in India between the academic social scientists and the administrators who are called upon to solve social problems. While the academic theorists look upon the work of the administrators with suspicion and even undervalue its

Preface

relevance to fundamental research, the administrators have tended to look upon the work of academic men as useless for their purpose. Both are mistaken. This study should show that academic research of a fundamental theoretical type depends upon data which may be of crucial value in application. The two must go hand in hand. Although the main stress here is on formulating theoretical concepts, administrators will find here material of great relevance to their work. This is a comparative study because today the village is being drawn into the larger, wider society which is eventually the world society.

The Indian administrators today have embarked on a programme of fundamental social change, and they need to understand the basic urges, values and dynamics of the traditional society if they are to change it. It is hoped that this study will be a helpful contribution towards the solution of such a problem. It was found that the villagers cherished as most precious their traditional values and considered those who disregarded them as foreigners and even exploiters. This is not to say that they do not want any change. They are aware of the need for change, and they want to move with the rest of the world. In Shivapur, this can be seen in the fact that the older system and the new system coexist in the realms of law, economy, politics, hygiene, etc. However, while accepting the new, the village never gives up the old outright. It is this coexistence of change and continuity that gives the village its distinctive personality. Thus it happens that the key theme of this study is precisely change and continuity. If one is to improve the village society, one must go about in a scientific manner. But this by itself is not enough. One must show tact, understanding, sympathy and imagination while attempting to introduce improvements.

K. ISHWARAN

York University, Toronto,
Canada,
November, 1965.

I

THE SCENE

SHIVAPUR IS ONE of the many villages which dot the
territory of Mysore State, itself one of the 17 states of the
Indian federation. It is one of the biggest villages in one of
the biggest districts of the county of Dharwar. It is hardly
five minutes' walk from the Poona-Bangalore main road,
a busy communication line, busy round the clock. The
short path branching off from the trunk road is symbolic of
the new village scene: the path of bullock-carts (*chakkadi*),
horse-drawn cabs (*tonga*), trucks, jeeps and motor-cars.
The old and the new jostle each other, while continuity
and change coexist. About half-a-mile to the south-east of
Shivapur there is a railway station, named after the village,
and boding a busy industrial future for the area. The village
is sandwiched between the towns of Hubli and Dharwar,
now joined into a single area. Dharwar is primarily an
educational and cultural centre, a University town. It is also
the administrative headquarters of the district, presided
over by the district officer, designated as the Deputy Com-
missioner. It has a broadcasting station. Its population and
houses are widely scattered over an almost hilly terrain.
Thus it has a distinctly rural flavour. Hubli is quite a
contrast to it. Although it too has educational institutions,
it is essentially a commercial town. Its larger population
is packed to congestion. It has a clearly industrial air about
it. Shivapur has easy access to both these centres, and the
village itself is expected to be included in the corporation
area in the near future.

As one enters Shivapur through the short link road con-

necting the village to the trunk road, one sees on the left
the new school building (built in 1956), which is strictly
outside the traditional gate of entrance (*Agasi Bagilu*). The
well, the tank and the *Panchayat* office are also outside this
door and to one's left as one proceeds towards the village.
The new buildings have red tiles and they are the only ones
to possess this new look. The village is cut into twelve
streets, named after particular castes, their elevation, the
names of village officers and servants, the names of landlords
and of dominant lineages. There are 631 households which,
in all, amount to a population of 3,809, according to our own
census taken in 1961. There are three main religious groups
—the Hindu, the Jain and the Muslim. There are 13 castes,
further sub-divided into 40 sub-castes, all hierarchically
arranged. The Lingayats, the Marathas and the Muslims
(who function more or less as a caste) are the major castes in
that order. The Lingayats hold the major portion of the land,
and the Muslims, mostly landless, act as a balancing group
between the other two. Many of the Muslims seek jobs
outside the village.

How is Shivapur linked with the outside world? It was
not isolated before the advent of modern communications.
People from the village had gone out, sometimes as far as
seven hundred miles, on pilgrimages, for marriage purposes
or to attend festivals and fairs. But now there are modern
communications. The changes that have taken place may be
dramatically illustrated by referring to the experiences of
an old inhabitant of the village. This old man of about 75
remembers that when he was a young man he could hardly
count one motor vehicle in three hours. Now it is very
different. Almost every five minutes one can see a truck,
a car or a jeep rush past the village on the nearby trunk
road. The government buses which ply between Dharwar
and Hubli at the rate of one every twenty minutes serve the
village. There are buses which go to the village itself, and
these make five trips a day. They are usually full. One of the
villagers, the biggest landlord, owns a car, but he actually

lives in Dharwar, from whence he visits the village daily to look after his land interests. There are as many as sixty bicycles owned by the villagers. School-going children use them mostly, and the poorer ones usually walk. Though many villagers do use modern transport, a substantial number still prefer to walk. There are occasional trucks which go to the village. But in spite of all these modern transport conveniences the traditional bullock-cart still dominates the communications system of the village. It is used for all kinds of purposes, for going to the land, for attending the weekly markets, and marriages. Indeed, it is hardly possible to think of Shivapur without its procession of gaily decorated bullock-carts. It is still the proud symbol of a successful farmer. It is interesting that the nearby railway station does not figure among the important transport agencies of the village. Hardly two or three inhabitants, if that many, use it. There is a small post office which does not look too busy. According to our information, the local postmaster hardly has transactions exceeding Rs. 10/- a week. There are virtually no telegrams received at Shivapur or sent from it. Shivapur keeps itself abreast of the larger world outside with the help of two daily newspapers and two weekly papers, all in the local language, Kannada. All the eight tea-shops in the village get these papers, which are read by the visiting customers. There are two radio sets in the village, one owned by the village Panchayat, a statutory body, and the other by the local grocer. Both are run on a dry battery, since the village is as yet without any supply of electric power.

Shivapur is at the mercy of the vagaries of the monsoon for its water, whether for irrigation or for drinking. The rainfall figures for the last three years (1961–1963) underscore this point. In 1961, there was a rainfall of 1082·40 millimetres as against 654·57 for 1962 and 735·15 for 1963. The average rainfall for these years was 824·4 millimetres. Shivapur has three seasons. The rainy season begins in May and ends towards the close of October. The month of July sees the harvest rainfall, and this was 112·5 millimetres for 1963. The winter lasts from November to February. It is a very mild winter indeed, the temperature normally not falling below 13° C. Lastly, there is a summer from March to June, also very mild, the highest temperature registered being 38·09° C. Thus, it has an equable climate, with no sharp extremes. The soil of Shivapur is mixed, consisting of many varieties ranging from grey to brown to black. It is generally very fertile. The area of the village itself is 62·35 acres and the cultivatable land available is 5621·25 acres. It is hardly sufficient for the population, since as many as 40 per cent of the villagers are without land. The scarcity of the land available for cultivation is perhaps responsible for the fierce attachment of the villagers to it. Land, along with cattle, is highly valued by the folk of Shivapur. Land and cattle stand for prestige, honour and prosperity.

The economy of Shivapur is essentially traditional, being dominated by agriculture. The agricultural economy of the village is traditional since traditional patterns of cultivation are dominant. The consumption pattern is traditional. The implements used, the methods of cultivation adopted, the household ornaments used, etc., are all traditional. The housing system is traditional and tied to the economic class of the owner. The farmers may be divided into upper (those owning above 25 acres), middle (those owning between 24 and 12 acres), and lower (those owning less than 12 acres). All houses except ten are of mud. These ten are of stone. The upper-class house has a large verandah. The cattle which are so much a part of the life of the farmers of all classes are housed on both sides of the verandah. The doors are made of ornate wood, and iron bars are often used. There is a kitchen, a worshipping place, a store room and a back-yard. The middle-class habitation has a smaller verandah, and the cattle are kept to only one side of it, usually the right-hand side. There is a raised platform on its left. There is a kitchen, and a backyard where fodder is stocked. The lower-class house, which is much smaller, has no verandah.

The upper-class homes have bullock-carts, and the middle-class ones sometimes do. The lower-class usually have none. The upper classes normally own three or more pairs of bullocks, the middle two to three, and the lower only one. There are special bullock-carts with iron wheels, which are used ceremonially for carting the harvests. These are symbols of prestige, and owned by the wealthiest. In Shivapur there are only three of them. But these may be borrowed. The upper-class farmer invariably possesses a full set of agricultural implements, and the other classes sometimes borrow them from the upper-class farmers. The farmers are so deeply attached to their bullocks that they name them after their dead parents. The cow is generally regarded as sacred, but is not usually owned. The buffalo is the lactating animal. But the milk is sold, mostly for hotels in Dharwar. There are agents who handle the sale of milk. The feed for cattle is poor, there being no meadowland. Only during the months from July to December are they fed well, and from March to May they are virtually starved, with neither adequate grass nor water.

The main crops are paddy, wheat, jowar, cotton and pulses. Fruits are also grown, namely mangoes, limes, guavas and grapes. While the other crops are mostly used up for internal consumption, the fruits are cash crops. Shivapur is linked even with distant Bombay, which is a market for its mangoes. The fruits are usually sold in the nearby towns of Dharwar and Hubli. From mid-June to mid-July the farmers sow the kharif crops of paddy, ground nuts, millet, cereals and wheat. From August to September they weed and till for the rabi crops, wheat, cotton and cereals. From October to November they gather their kharif harvest and sow the rabi crops. From December to mid-February the harvesting of the kharif crop is completed. From mid-February to mid-March they collect the rabi harvest. From March to June is the time of leisure, for festivals and fairs, for feasting and weddings. The production and consumption pattern is, as can be seen, traditional. The idea of a cash crop prevails only in the case of horticulture, and even here the traditional approach is not entirely absent. For instance, recently a person who grew grapes distributed them within the village in the customary manner. Other crops are generally consumed by the village itself. At the time of the harvesting, whatever remains of the old stock in the storing pit is sold in the market, and the money thus obtained is used to buy clothing and ornaments, foodstuffs which are not grown in Shivapur, and other necessaries.

The traditional payment pattern still continues. The payment for services to artisans is still made in kind. Every week the villagers sell grain and buy the necessaries they require such as soap, sugar, jaggery, tea, etc. The priest of their caste is presented with a portion of the harvested grain as a gesture of thanks to the powers beyond. Then follows the gift to the ritual dignitaries who have officiated during the harvesting ceremony. Thus all are paid in kind.

While every fourth household depends on agriculture, every eighth household depends on labour. Three-fourths of the population is involved in agriculture, and one-fourth is landless labour. Every 21st family is an artisan family. Only eight families practise sheep-rearing. Every tenth family depends on trade, buying or selling groceries, corn and other retail consumer goods. The artisan class is a specialised class which seeks emotional and economic security in its work.

It is interesting to note that the primary school was started as far back as 1868 and the urdu school as far back as 1895. Thus though interest in education appeared early, there has been virtually no development in terms of an educational institution. This points to a lack of interest in the education of children.

Speaking in terms of heads of families, it was found that, of the 631 heads, as many as 364, or about 58 per cent, were illiterate. As many as 598 heads had not completed their primary education. Only 29 of them had reached the secondary level. Five had been to college, and only one had had post-graduate education. Under the state law, primary education is compulsory for all children between the ages of 6 and 11. Shivapur has a primary school, which, for lack of space, has been split up into two wings, one located in the eastern part of the village and the other in the western. There is also an urdu school, located in the Muslim area, and 100 per cent of its students are Muslim, as are its two teachers. In the primary school there are 527 pupils on the rolls. But this is due to the requirement of the law. The actual attendance is round about 300. And even this number is unreliable since a student's name, once entered, continues from class to class irrespective of the fact of his non-attendance. The children of the artisans constitute the most regular absentees. Those of the labour class come next in the extent to which they are absent from school. During the harvest season they are completely absent. While children of untouchables and the higher castes mix within the walls of the school, once outside, the distance between them is resumed. Less than 10 per cent of the girls are at school. In fact girls do not go to school after the age of 10. On the attitude to the education of girls, an incident may be cited. The daughter of a schoolmistress at the primary school who went to college, was chased out by village boys. Eventually the poor teacher had to live away from the village.

Regarding the pattern of further education, it is found that only about 30 boys belonging to the upper- and middle-class farm families go up for secondary education at Dharwar. About 10 go to college. There is no Holeya (untouchable), Kuruba (shepherd) or Maratha student pursuing education beyond the village. The upper classes do not as a rule send their children outside Shivapur for further education. The village has to date produced two lawyers (father and son), one medical practitioner (M.B.B.S.), and one science teacher at a college. The fact that the majority of the heads are illiterate has had its impact on the educational pattern. On the one hand, this must be considered a major reason why the girls are denied education. On the other

hand, the realisation that education led to no relevant purpose or function in the village must have discouraged
school-going, whatever the law might demand. Moreover,
the unemployment situation for the uneducated must have
influenced the thinking of the highly pragmatic villagers.

The Hindu view of life permeates the whole ethos of
Shivapur, not excluding its religion. This gives it a certain
integrated personality, in spite of certain obvious differences
between groups. The three main religious groups are the
Hindu, the Jain and the Muslim, although the last of these
functions as a caste group as well. Though in matters of
theology and doctrine these groups may differ, yet they are
knit together into a single working system, thanks to the
all-pervasive Hindu outlook. Thus one may see how all
three groups resemble one another with regard to their
value system and ritualistic forms. All of them hold the
familiar Hindu belief in the value system of four fundamental goals: the *Dharma* (duty, morality, law, etc., all
combined in one), *Artha* (material welfare), *Kama* (physical
love), and *Moksha* (spiritual salvation); and in the division
of human life into the four stages (Ashrams) of life: the
bachelor, the householder, the mendicant and the ascetic.
The *rites of passage* adopted by all three groups are dominated
by Hindu themes and motives. So far as the boys are concerned, these rites include the birth and initiation ceremony,
the naming ceremony, the tonsure ceremony, the ear-boring
ceremony, marriage and funeral rites. So far as the girls are
concerned, they are the birth, naming, ear-boring, nose-
boring, puberty, marriage, pregnancy and funeral rites. Even
with regard to their festivals, there are common events.
While it is true that each of them has developed festivals
unique to itself, there are nevertheless festivals which,
though nominally associated with one of them, belong to
all and in which the entire village community participates.

The unique festivals are the *Ramzan* for Muslims, the
Basava Jayanti fot the Lingayats, the *Shiva Jayanti* for the
Marathas, the *Birappa* festival for the Kurubas and the

Mayevva festival for the Holeyas. The common festivals are the *Moharrum*, the *Karahunnime*, the *Holi*, the *Nagarapan-chime*, the *Ugadi*, the *Ganapati* and the *Dyamavva* festivals. In short, with regard to religion the village presents a common profile.

The political life of Shivapur, as in the case of almost every human society, manifests itself at two levels, the formal and the informal. The village council (*Grama Pan-chayati*), a statutory body, is the symbol as well as the actuality of formal political activities of the village. The village council or *Panchayati* elections were introduced first in 1949, followed by three subsequent elections in 1953, 1957 and 1960, respectively. It is to the point here to re-capitulate what happened in these elections. In the first election there was little organised campaigning, and a Lingayat who was a village landlord belonging to one of the important lineages of headmen was elected as Chairman. In the 1953 election, with the considerable advance in political consciousness as represented by increased ability in political organisation and strategy, there was a real contest in which a Maratha candidate was returned, interestingly enough with the support of the faction-ridden Lingayats themselves. In the 1957 election, a Maratha candidate got in by a large majority. The 1960 election was expected to be keenly contested, and the presence of the police during the election was considered necessary in view of apprehended violence. In this closely and bitterly fought battle the Lingayat candidate emerged victorious. Roughly, these and like happenings may be designated as the content of formal politics.

The broad structure of informal politics which underpins the formal may be now sketched. From this point of view the village streets are divided into those revolving round caste loyalties, those revolving round occupational loyalties and those revolving round mixed loyalties. The key institution of normal politics, the council of elders, reflects three levels of political activities. Firstly, there is a council of elders organised on the basis of caste. Secondly, there is a council of elders organised on the basis of the street. Lastly, there is the council of elders organised on the basis of the village as a whole. The units of political loyalty involved here are the caste (*Jati*), the street (*oni*), and the village (*uru*). The strength of political loyalty decreases as it proceeds from the caste to the village, the former being the most intense and the latter the least. The Holeyas have a caste council but no street council. Needless to say there is overlapping between these organisations. The really important tussle in the political arena is between the informal (that is, in the sense of being extra-legal) caste council (*Jati Panchayati*), and the formal village council (*Grama Panchayati*). The former has been legally divested of most of its powers. For instance, it no longer enjoys the very important power of excommunication. Yet in terms of what we have called informal politics, it is very dominant. Any decision on its part to withdraw co-operation from a person is regarded as a serious handicap since, in practice, it reduces the individual to a helpless position. The reason for this is that the caste Panchayat has deep roots in the traditions and modes of the people: its leadership, which is widely and without contest generally accepted, is hereditary.

In sharp contrast to it, the village Panchayat, the pinnacle of formal politics, derives its authority from a contest, is impersonal, and has no genuine roots in popular life. It roughly approximates the Weberian category of the rational-impersonal. It is a secular and money-collecting agency, and evokes no really enthusiastic response from the village folk. Thus the political life of Shivapur is characterised by a basic dichotomy between these levels—the caste and the secular-modern. The personnel of the two levels of politics are not the same. For instance, it is observed that the caste leaders are not always electorally successful. None the less their influence on the political decisions of the village is very important.

The dichotomy noticed in the political life has a parallel in the legal system of Shivapur. This is no accident, since the legal and the political are deeply interconnected realms.

Shivapur may be described as bilegal. If law is regarded as a mode of social control, then in Shivapur two systems coexist. There is the customary law and there is the modern positive law. The villagers resort to both as and when it suits them. As between the two systems, a clear dominance of the customary law is noticeable. The attitudes of the villagers to the two systems are significant. It has been said that the general opinion of the villagers is that the settling of disputes through customary law and its agencies is proper, whereas resorting to the law courts is not worthy. The customary law is closely related to the all-pervasive concept of *Dharma*. Thus one can notice how the legal order is part of a wider social, even cosmic order. The sanctions of customary law are both social censure and divine punishment. The customary law is necessarily complicated, not being uniformly relevant to all groups. Also, it has spread its tentacles into areas of life where modern law can hardly penetrate. The customary law recognises all kinds of disputes—public and private. In the former kind of dispute the offence is considered to be against the community, while in the latter it is against a private party. The application of the customary public law is not uniform since it takes into account the character, status, role and personality of the offender.

The sharp contrast posited between the customary and the modern law does not obtain in Shivapur. In fact, the modern law has recognised the central role of customary law in the life of the people, and no less an authority than the Indian Supreme Court has declared that '. . . under the Hindu System of Law clear proof of usages will outweigh the written text'. The two systems have a working relationship, though, as already pointed out, the villagers themselves prefer the customary to the modern law. Thus the legal realm, as indeed the totality of life in Shivapur, is a scene of tradition as well as change—in which there is a profound continuity of institutions and values as well as innovation.

II

SOCIAL STRUCTURE

A CASUAL LOOK at the social structure of Shivapur is apt to give one a misleadingly simple pattern—an impression reinforced by the great simplicity of the material culture of the people. If one probes deeper, one discovers a situation bristling with complexities. The complexity of the social structure could be easily illustrated with reference to the institutions of caste, religion, economy, kinship and marriage.

It is appropriate to begin an examination of the social structure with the caste system as it obtains in Shivapur, since it is the very foundation on which the rest of the structure has been built. The basic principle of the caste system is hierarchy. Its basic unit is the sub-caste, since it is the smallest endogamous social unit. Historically, the *Varna* institution through a process of inter-mixing became the *Jati* (caste), and the *Jati* has further split up into the *upa-Jati* (sub-caste), which may be considered a unit more fundamental than the *Jati*. While it is profitable, and even necessary, to keep in mind the general model of the classic five-fold *Varna* system of the *Brahmana, Kshatriya, Vaishya, Sudra* and the *untouchable,* it is important not to identify it too easily with local patterns. In Shivapur there is nothing exactly corresponding to the *Kshatriya* caste. Historically, the classical *Varna* system has never existed in practice in its pristine purity.

The caste is an institution whose membership is governed by the principles of birth, endogamy, occupation, purity and pollution, distance, inter-dining and drinking, in that order.

16

The specific contents of the classic model of the *Varna* system is not of universal application, but its principles are. In Shivapur, its basic principles operate in all the crucial areas of the social system. Each caste and sub-caste group is, to some extent, an isolated island with its own patterns of behaviour and values, though all of them are related to a larger social structure. The fundamental principle of hierarchy governs this larger structure. But hierarchy is at the same time both a subjective phenomenon involving the attitudes of the people themselves and an objective phenomenon which an outsider can observe as revealed in the behaviour patterns of the people. Though in the classic caste model, the Brahmana is supposed to be the highest caste, in our observation this is not true of Shivapur. Here, it is the Lingayats who are the highest group, both in terms of subjective popular attitudes and our objective appraisal of their behaviour.

The lower status of the Brahmana may be attributed to several causes. In the first place, the local Brahmans have suffered economic degradation. Secondly, they are no longer considered faithful adherents to their own ritualistic rules and practices. For instance, quite contrary to their caste mandates, they have taken to self-cultivation of land, in order to counteract the tenancy laws which rule out absentee landlordism. Also they are believed by the people to have degraded themselves by officiating as priests at lower caste ceremonies. Educationally, too, they have been no better off. It is significant that the village teachers belong to the Lingayat, not Brahmana caste. The superiority of the Lingayat, in consequence, may be attributed to his economic, ritualistic, occupational and educational status.

Perhaps at this point we may introduce the subject of what has been called 'the dominant caste'. In our study it was found that this concept is misleading, unless substantially modified. It has been observed by us that whenever one caste tends to become too dominant, the other groups tend to combine to maintain some kind of balance of power. We have also found it necessary to question a subsidiary notion, namely that the lower castes tend to imitate the 'dominant' caste. It is true that castes tend to take over features from other castes, but one is unable to see how this is essentially connected with the idea of dominance. It is preferable to invoke the ideas of culture contact and reference group. The key notion is not simple dominance or imitation, it is contact. This alone would explain adequately the extraordinary resistance the caste groups offer to any introduction of outside features, and also the infrequency and slowness of such incorporations.

We may now proceed to map the social structure with its castes and sub-castes. Castes are dealt with here in the order of their status, hierarchically. For reasons elsewhere discussed, we propose to assign to the Lingayats the top place in the caste hierarchy as it operates in Shivapur. The Lingayat caste is numerically the largest, and there are 187 households belonging to it. It is further sub-divided into the following sub-castes in order of descending status:

1 Hiremath
2 Chikkamath
3 Ganachari
4 Mathapati
5 Hugar
6 Pujar
7 Banajiga:
    a. Adi Banajiga
    b. Sheelavant Banajiga
8 Panchamasali
9 Panchamasali Totiga
10 Sadar
11 Jadar:
    a. Bile Jadar
    b. Kare Jadar

12 Ganiga:
    a. Bile Ganiga
    b. Kare Ganiga
13 Hadapad

In this hierarchy the top level comprises the priestly sub-castes which run down to Pujar. The Hiremath and the Chikkamath are at the top of the priestly group themselves. Both trace their origin from great antiquity. The Hiremath is believed to be the oldest lineage, and hence its superiority. A Ganachari is equal to a priest but he is not expected to officiate at religious ceremonies. However, he may conduct worship in the temple. The Mathapati may also perform the *puja* (worship) at the temple. In Shivapur he worships the Basava (Bull-God) at the temple atop a small hillock near the village. He is employed in sending marriage invitations. He is also the person to wash the feet of the priest while they are placed on a dead man's body. He, unlike a Ganachari, acts as a secretary to the priest. The Hugar is not quite a member of the priestly corpus, but he has duties associated with it. He is, so to say, on the priestly fringe. He is a florist occupationally and hence he is important to religious ceremonies. He is the man who prepares the lovely wedding crown of flowers. He is the man who announces authoritatively the dates of festivals. The relationship between the Banajiga and the Panchamasali is governed by religious status, occupational purity and pollution. In terms of the latter, the Banajiga ranks higher than the Panchamasali. The former observes rules of pollution strictly in relation to the latter. In the same manner the Panchamasali observe rules of pollution in relation to the next group. Among the Banajigas, the Adi Banajigas are higher in status than the Sheelavant Banajigas, since the former trace their antiquity to an earlier period than the latter. Occupationally, the Banajigas are tradesmen, mostly functioning as village grocers. The Panchamasali sub-caste is, occupationally, similar to the Banajiga and the Sadars. The Panchamasali Totiga specialises in gardening.

These groups differ on the ground that they trace descent from different lineage heads.

The Sadars are Lingayats who practise the *udiki* system in which widow/widower marriage is permissible. The Jadars are the weavers, and among them there are two further wings, the Bile (white) Jadaru and the Kare (black) Jadaru. The Bile (white) Jadaru weave white cloth which is used by men, and the Kare Jadaru weave black cloth or the saree which is worn by women. The Bile Jadaru are superior to the Kare Jadaru presumably for this reason. This distinction which is partly one of colour, though primarily one of sex evaluation, may be of interest to those interested in the colour in general. The Ganigas who manufacture the oil needed by the village are also divided into the Bile (white) and Kare (black) wings. Again here the Bile wing is superior to the Kare wing. The superiority of the Bile Ganigas derives from the fact that they do not practise the *udiki* while the Kare Jadars do. It may be mentioned that the *udiki* is generally looked upon as an undesirable thing by the villagers. The lowest in the Lingayat hierarchy is the Hadapad sub-caste which performs the function of the barbers. Hence it involves pollution, and as a result has been pushed down to the bottom of the scale. A general comment may be made here that the sub-caste is an endogamous unit, identified with occupation.

The Brahmana caste is numerically the smallest. There are only five Brahmana households divided into two sub-castes, Vaishnava and Smartha. The former is considered superior to the latter, as indicated by the fact that a girl from the Smartha marries a Vaishnava whereas a girl from the Vaishnava seldom does. The traditional superiority of the Brahmana in the classic *varna* model does not hold good in Shivapur. Socially, he has suffered a lowering of status in relation to the Lingayats; the reasons for this state of affairs have already been suggested.

The Jains come next. They have forty-four households. In hierarchy they are the third. They are divided into the sub-castes, the Digambara and the Svetambar. The former are considered superior to the latter as they embody more fully the Jaina ideal of renunciation. They are supposed to have given up wearing clothes as that would harm other lives. The Svetambars are allowed to wear clothes. They are regarded here as a caste, as are the Muslims, since the social function of these groups within the social frame of Shivapur is that of a caste.

The Vaishyas have five households. They are grocers and tradesmen. They are vegetarians, and their role in Shivapur approximates the classic model.

Next come the Panchals, the artisan caste. Within this caste there are further rankings based on occupation. Among them the Badiga (carpenter) ranks lower only to the Pattar (goldsmith). Wood, which is earlier ethnologically than metal, is considered of a higher status than metal, and the Pattar's superiority may be explained by the value attached to his skill. It is significant that the images of village god-esses are carved out of wood or stone. Next to them come the Kambar (ironsmith). His superiority to the Shilpi (stone-sculptor) may be accounted for by his utility to the com-munity. The Shilpi who comes next is supposed to be superior to the Kanchagar (the brass-worker). There are in all 13 panchal households in the village.

The Marathas have 129 households and are numerically the second most important caste. They are divided into four sub-castes: Buruki, the Jande Rawut, the Kulavadi and the Nadakattu, in that order. The Buruki, whose name has associations with Burqui (or the 'Parada'), practise the *Parada* system in which women are veiled. They are the only Marathas to practise it. This custom may be explained as indicating the importance attached to women in that sub-caste. They are to be secluded and protected since they are so precious. The Jande Rawuts are so called because they are believed to have descended from the soldiers carrying flags under Shivaji, the great Maratha chieftain and empire-builder. The Kulavadis and the Nadukattis are recent converts, and the superiority of the former to the latter is explained by the fact that they are earlier converts. The Marathas eat meat, cultivate land on a small scale or work as landless labourers, and take to servility. Their meat-eating along with their work as menial servants must have been responsible for their rank so low down in the hierarchy.

The Rajaput caste which is numerically negligible is divided into two groups, Singh and Kayastha. The former claims to have royal blood in its veins and, therefore, to be superior to the latter.

The Kurubas are traditionally shepherds, but now are mainly agriculturists. The Kuruba caste is divided into the Hattikankan and the Unnikankan. The Hattikankan Kurubas are so called because they wear bangles of cotton, and the Unnikankans get their name from the fact that they wear bangles of wool. The implication is that cotton is superior to wool, the reason perhaps being that cotton reflects a more settled society whereas wool a more nomadic one. The Kurubas are usually the official servants of the village. They are small agriculturists and they produce the hand-woven woollen blanket (*kambali*). They eat meat. There are as many as 77 Kuruba households in Shivapur.

The Muslims are the third largest numerically since there are 113 of their households. Politically they perform the function of balancing the conflict between the other major castes of the Lingayat and the Maratha. They are divided into four sub-castes, 1. the Sheikh, 2. the Sayad, 3. the Moghal, 4. the Pathan, in that order. The Sheikh, the priestly class, tops the hierarchy. They are believed to have descended from the Prophet. The Sayad is the lower priest, and he cannot conduct the rituals of the group. The Moghals are believed to have descended from the ruling dynasty of the Moghals, while the Pathans are supposed to have come from Afghanistan. The fact that they are both immigrants may explain their lower status.

The Barikars are the village servants, whose services are called in during feasts and festivals of the village as well as of individual families. They clean the pots and pans on such occasions, attend to the cattle of the guests, and perform similar odd jobs.

The Talawars too, are village servants. They are hunters as well, and cultivate on a very small scale.

The Korava are the village instrumental musicians whose services are requisitioned on public as well as private occasions. They make bamboo baskets and brooms which are sold in Dharwar market and neighbouring villages. Right down at the bottom of the caste scale come the Holeya, the untouchables. There are 23 households belonging to them. They are further divided into sub-groups of the Cheluvadis, the local Madiga and the immigrant Madiga, in that order. Their lowest ranking is due to the pollution institution. The Cheluvadis do not eat the flesh of dead animals; however, they skin the dead animals, and give the skin to the Madigas, who make shoes out of it for the village. The custom is that the Cheluvadis first take the dead animal, and pass it on to the Madigas who eat the flesh of the animal after skinning. Their superiority lies in the fact that they do not eat the flesh of dead animals, whereas Madigas do. Among the Madigas, the Iddur (local) Madigas rank higher than the Parauru (immigrant) Madigas. The Cheluvadis are village sweepers and are used in sending messages about the dead, and the Madigas play the funeral drum.

While the above account has dealt with the castes in a vertical hierarchical perspective, it is suggested that the castes may be brought under six broad groupings:

1 Lingayat, Brahmana, Jain, Vaishya and the Panchal,
2 Maratha and Rajaput
3 Kuruba
4 Muslim
5 Barikar, Talawar and Korava
6 Holeya

They may be placed hierarchically in the following way:

CASTE HIERARCHY

Grouping	Caste
I	1 Lingayat 2 Brahman 3 Jain 4 Vaishya 5 Panchal
II	6 Maratha 7 Rajaput
III	8 Kurub
IV	9 Muslim
V	10 Barikar 11 Talawar 12 Korava
VI	13 Holeya

The structure so far mapped is intimately connected with the concept of *Dharma* and *Karma*. The *Dharma* is a blanket word indicating all codes and rules of conduct governing a group. It is essentially an ethical concept. The *Dharma* is supposed to be the sustaining value underlying all group life, and, eventually, individual life. It is through his group that the individual realises his *Dharma*. The notion of *Karma* is also important as a social force. With it go the twin and complementary ideas of *Punya* (merit) and *Papa* (sin). These operate as sanctions of considerable force in the social dynamics of the village.

The model sketched above is not static, and indeed an eternally static social model is a myth. The pace of change, however, is very slow, though it tends to be increasingly faster. The Hindu Society, while it may change so slowly as to create an illusion of being static, has never been entirely static. The existence of a great variety of codes and customs within the broad Hindu frame-work is an adequate indication of this dynamic aspect of society. The institution of caste is a fine example in this connection. It has changed considerably but it has lost none of its *essential* functions. No doubt it has diversed itself of some secondary attributes. This explains why it persists. Unless it answered to some fundamental urge it would hardly have survived. But survival has a price, which is change. The change, as already noted, has been slow. So far, in Shivapur there have been only one inter-religious, five inter-caste and just one inter-sub-caste marriage in the last century or so. But there are further changes in other areas of life. The rules for dining and drinking water have been considerably relaxed. So also have the rules of purity and pollution. The former relaxation may be attributed to the modern modes of transport, the number of the tea-shops and the new egalitarian laws. In the olden days the bullock-cart would permit of a more rigid following of food and drink rules since one travelled in a closed group. But in modern transport one is thrown amidst strangers and one cannot afford to be strict. Even so, the relaxation is not complete. In Shivapur there are 11 tea-shops. The Holeyas are permitted into these places, but they must drink their tea from broken cups specially set apart for them, and must wash them. The role of the news-papers and the operation of government-sponsored Community Development projects have also contributed considerably to the relaxation of the ancient rules. One often feels, as in the case of the tea-shop example above, that the changes are more verbal than real, and that people speak in one language and act in quite another. Once again we are driven to our central theme—the village today is a scene of change as well as continuity. The old is discarded, but not wholly, and the new is welcomed, again not wholly. One may venture to say that Shivapur is a symbol of the new India emerging gradually, though unmistakably, out of the old India.

The picture of the social structure of Shivapur offered here will not be complete unless we take into consideration its five other dimensions: (1) the relationship between caste and occupation, (2) the relationship between caste and endogamy, (3) the relationship between caste and purity and pollution rules, (4) the relationship between caste, and the rules for commensality, and (5) the relationship between caste and distance.

Taking the first of these, it may be generally observed that there is an identification of caste with occupation. One is not only born into a caste but also to the occupation which is associated with that caste. Generally, the traditional occupations are followed, thus expressing an essentially conservative approach to the question of choosing one's occupation. However, most persons follow more than one occupation, of which the traditional occupation is primary. In addition to the primary occupation, there is also the practice of supplementing it by secondary, tertiary, etc., occupations. This multi-occupational pattern may be explained by the fact that the low-level economy of the village makes it necessary for persons to go outside the traditional occupations. It is possible to rank occupations in relation to individuals, and in relation to the society as a whole. So far as the individual is concerned, the traditional occupation ranks as primary, and the rest are followed in order of their economic importance to him. Taking the society as a whole, they are viewed hierarchically. The 21 occupations may be hierarchically arranged in order of their social status as follows:

1 Priest
2 Astrologer-cum-priest
3 Farmer and Headman
4 Florist
5 Goldsmith

6 Carpenter
7 Blacksmith
8 Weaver
9 Trader
10 Bangle-seller
11 Tea-shop owner
12 Oil seller
13 Shepherd
14 Village servant/labourer
15 Barber
16 Washerman
17 Basket-maker
18 Servant
19 Labourer
20 Sweeper
21 Leather worker

Though most persons are forced to supplement their traditional occupation with a side-line, the agriculturists of the upper and middle classes seldom feel the need for a secondary occupation. In their case, of course, it may be argued that they have a secondary occupation in the shape of marketing their produce, in addition to growing it. Thus one notices scope for occupational mobility within the framework of primary, traditional occupations. This must be qualified with the proviso that there are limits set to it by the opportunities within the village.

We have already indicated the hierarchical arrangement of the occupations. It remains now to explain the rationale of the arrangement. The priest is at the top, thus underscoring the traditional sense of values. The priest is invariably a poor farmer. This points to the fact that the determination of the status of an occupation depends on more than the economic factor. There is a connection between pollution and occupation. In this connection it may be observed that the Lingayats cherish highly the ideal of the dignity of labour. This is to be explained with reference to the historical antecedents of the Lingayat movement. Basava, the great social and religious reformer of the 12th century, spearheaded a vigorous popular revolt in Karnatak (the Kannada-speaking territory in which Shivapur is located) against the Brahmanical system. Basava preached the doctrine of *Kayaka*, implying the spiritual value of labour. The Lingayats, who are the products of this great movement, have naturally assigned to labour a place of central importance. It is no accident that the Lingayats are the only caste in Shivapur with a sub-caste specialising in the occupation of the barber.

It is interesting to note that when a person inherits his father's occupation, he also inherits his father's clients. Despite its outward impression of cheerfulness, Shivapur has its share of economic problems like poverty and unemployment. The agricultural and artisan family cannot absorb all their working members into their traditional occupations. Thus the redundant members are forced to seek work outside the village. This makes for some flexibility in the occupational system. But the most important thing to bear in mind in this context is that a certain fundamental moral propriety attaches to the occupation of one's parents. It is, in fact, considered one's *Dharma* to follow it. Hence those unable to do so always carry a sense of moral guilt with them. It is not so much that others may disapprove of them, but more that they themselves feel guilty. The Lingayats are the major farming group in the village. They own nearly three-fifths of the village land. They are economically well-off, and this is reflected in the conspicuous consumption in which they indulge. Their festivals, marriages and recreational activities are performed on an impressive and costly scale. Of the 697 persons in the village who depend exclusively on agriculture for their livelihood, 312 hail from the Lingayat caste. The Maratha agriculturists, who number 126, come next, and they make unsuccessful efforts to rival the Lingayats in conspicuous consumption. 84 Kurubas, 58 Muslims and 3 Brahmans depend for their livelihood solely on agriculture. Of the rest, 104 belong to other castes. Three-fourths of the Muslims, the Talawars, the Koravas and the Holeyas are landless. One-fourth of the Muslim population has taken to the occupation of the Washerman. Land is accorded the highest value by the villagers, and the landed are held in high esteem and occupy positions of power and prestige. Their doings form the main theme of village gossip. As many as 54 per cent of the Marathas lack enough land to make a living, and these are diverted to seek other jobs both within and outside the village. The Muslims are generally labourers. The artisans who are highly specialised do not, naturally, have scope for any secondary activity. Hence they are not farmers, with rare exceptions. One blacksmith and one carpenter family do farming, but their prestige derives not from the fact that they farm but from the fact that they own land. The other castes practise their traditional occupations, and take to farming as a secondary or tertiary occupation. The Lingayat priest attends to the religious needs of his community, as well as those of the Barikars, Kurubas, Talawars, Koravas and the Holeyas. The Brahmana priest is consulted by the Marathas, Kurubas and other low caste groups for the dates of auspicious occasions. No priest goes to the untouchable locality, but they send rice of blessing through somebody. The Rajputs have their own priest, an old man. The Jains go to their priests in Dharwar. The Muslims never go to a Hindu priest and have their own priests.

The rules of endogamy are generally adhered to with rigidity. This institution is preserved by various factors such as the nature of the locality. It may be recalled that in Shivapur streets normally run along caste and occupational lines. Thus physical proximity reinforces caste exclusiveness. In Shivapur village endogamy is more prevalent than in most villages. In the last 10 years or so there have been 20 endo-gamous marriages. Occupation, together with locality, strengthens the institution of endogamy. Mixed localities are forbidden, as they constitute a potential danger to endogamy. There is occupational endogamy within a caste group. A Lingayat farmer, for example, has marriage alliances with a Lingayat farmer. The Muslims are willing to marry from any family provided the new entrant is willing to be converted. Even among them the impact of caste endogamy is evident in the fact that Muslim washermen marry only Muslim washerwomen. There is not merely occupational endogamy: there is also what may be called economic endogamy. A family of upper-class farmers will have marriage alliances only with other farmers of upper-class farmers. It is noteworthy that education is rated the least important factor in matrimonial arrangements. Recently a young man with a post-graduate qualification in science working as a research assistant in a university laboratory found himself unacceptable in a marriage alliance because he possessed no landed property.

One observes in Shivapur the process of fragmentation of family lineages into smaller families. One may cite in this connection the examples of the Patil, Itigatti and Ballur families among the Lingayats, and the Mane and More families among the Marathas. The practice of cross-cousin and exchange marriage, as well as the joint-family system, tend to strengthen caste solidarity and unity. Of the 631 households interviewed, as many as 546 favoured the joint family. Only 70 favoured the elementary family. 13 were indifferent, and 2 declared they did not know the answer.

So far as purity and pollution rules go, one notices now that there has been a modification, mainly in response to economic or material circumstances. The situation does not follow the Brahmana model in which the rules are blindly and rigidly followed. Apart from the Brahmans, only the Jains follow them in Shivapur. The economically well-to-do farmers make a show act of the puberty rite, but the motive here is not so much ritualistic as conspicuous consumption. Pollution rules associated with birth are modified by economic circumstances. Regarding death, the rule is that if one dies at an inauspicious time, the house must be vacated.

But in Shivapur good houses are scarce, and such a rule is impossible to follow in practice. So there is a symbolic vacation for a night or so, and the party returns soon after. In the temples, the Holeyas and the Muslims are not admitted. In a Muslim mosque any one may enter. The Holeyas may not offer cooked food as an offering in the temples. The Muslims and the low-caste Hindus like the Talawars, etc., may not offer cooked food to the gods of the high-caste Hindus. The days of worship are listed according to a clear-cut religious calendar. For the Lingayats, Monday and Friday are worship days. For the Marathas, they are Tuesday, Wednesday and Sunday. For the Jains and Kurubas, it is Tuesday, and for the Talawars, it is Saturday. For the artisans, it is Friday, and for the Muslims, Thursday. On Monday, *Basavanna* is worshipped; on Tuesday and Thursday *Allah;* on Friday *Karevva, Durgavva* and *Mayevva;* on Saturday *Hanumantha;* and on Sunday *Khandobha.* These days can also be divided into male or female days, depending on the deities. Only on these days do the farmers take a bath.

There has been considerable relaxation in the rules governing commensality. For instance, 25 years ago there was no commensality between the Lingayat sub-castes. There is a story that in those days a Banajiga who came to Shivapur to attend a wedding would not accept food from his Sadar host and had to get it from a Hiremath family. Now, so far as the sub-castes are concerned, this has disappeared among all castes. However, as between castes, it still operates. The higher castes will not accept food and water from a lower. Formerly even as between sub-castes it operated. A man from another sub-caste would not touch the water-pot on its way from the tank. Nowadays a member of a sub-caste is allowed to do it. Even a member of the Maratha caste is permitted to help a Lingayat in positioning a water pitcher on the head. A Muslim, however, is not allowed to do it if the water is meant for human consumption. When a Muslim helps in such a situation, it may be taken for granted that the water is meant for the use of cattle. Apart from the common tank, each caste has its own well. The common tank is resorted to usually only when there is water scarcity. It is noteworthy that the Holeyas are never allowed to use the common tank as the opinion of the village community as a whole is overwhelmingly against it. When a higher caste man pours water for drinking into the cupped palm of a lower caste man, he always does it from a considerable height.

If one takes into account public places, the distinctions between castes and sub-castes have largely disappeared. This may be demonstrated with reference to the tea-shop. The tea-shop is a great social leveller. Yet links with the older system are not entirely absent. What is perhaps most important, there is no conscious effort of any strength worth mentioning to break the caste distinctions. Such breaches as occur are forced by circumstances. It is also significant that the lower castes themselves do not appear to be too eager to break them. Recently a village elder of high caste frequented a tea-shop in nearby Dharwar. At about the same time a Holeya from the village was also there to take tea. As soon as he felt the gaze of the elder, the Holeya felt a sense of guilt and left the tea-shop abruptly.

There are other interesting points to note about the purity and pollution rules. After shaving one is supposed to be impure and one is not to be touched. During the period of menstruation a woman is not allowed to touch babies. A family in which a marriage has taken place does not observe the *Karahunnime* festival during the first year after the marriage. While fetching water the Brahmans strictly follow the rule of not touching anybody. The Lingayats take the help only of Lingayats in positioning their water pitcher, whereas the Brahmans do not take any help from anybody. All non-Brahmans take help from Lingayats on such occasions. The Marathas take help from the Marathas and the Lingayats, but not from the Talawars and the Kurubas. The Muslims take help from all excepting the Talawars, the Koravas and the Holeyas. The Jains take such help only from the Lingayats. The Brahmans, the Vaishyas, the Panchalas and the Rajputs do not touch anybody while fetching water. Perhaps these castes adhere to rules of purity and pollution so rigidly as a means of asserting their status against its lowering in terms of other factors, say, the economic. When a Brahman serves tea at his home to members of other castes, he either asks them to clean the cups or has them cleaned by his servants.

The problem of distance may be discussed with reference to the home, the school, the *Math* (religious establishment), public places like the tea-shop and the Panchayat office, and occasions like the harvests and other ceremonial events. The Holeyas are not permitted full access to the homes of the high-castes. At best they are allowed to go through the outer passage of the house. The Barikar, the Korava and the Talawar are allowed to sit on the platform opposite to the place where the cattle are kept. But they are not allowed to sit with their feet tucked up. They must cross their legs. Among the Lingayat sub-castes, persons belonging to the groups up to the Pujar are allowed free access into the god's place, and when the sub-castes below that level are allowed, it is with considerable hesitation. However, only the priests are permitted to eat there. There is a strong feeling among the inhabitants of Shivapur that a violation of such rules would be punished with the visitation of snakes, scorpions, and dangerous or unpleasant insects. The castes which eat meat, the Marathas and the Kurubas, are not allowed into the kitchen and the god's place. At school children do mix, though they do not accept eatables from the Holeyas. But once out of the four walls of the school, the high-caste children take a ritual wash. In the temples the Holeyas are not allowed.

In public places, for instance, during meetings convened by visiting or local officials, the caste hierarchy is symbolically represented in the seating arrangements. The higher the caste status of a person, the closer he is seated to the guest. In the pattern of local of temples, the same theme is repeated.

The temples of the high-castes are located nearer the heart of Shivapur, and those of the other, in proportion to their status, are located away from the centre. The Holeyas have their temples in their own area. The Muslim mosque is located near the area of the Holeyas, thus underlining its inclusiveness. The Lingayats, the Brahmans and the Marathas do not touch a Holeya. While worshipping, they do not touch other members of their own castes. The physical contiguation of Shivapur represents in its own manner the social contiguation. The one reinforces the other in subtle ways. In the tea-shops the Holeyas are not allowed to sit on the wooden benches or the raised earthen platforms. They are expected to squat on the ground and to take tea from broken cups. During the harvest time, the Holeyas are employed up to the time when the thrashing-floor is prepared. Thereafter their services are systematically dispensed with. This has to be explained by the fact that the idea of pollution would not permit of the employment of Holeyas where food material is concerned. The best and the top layers of the grain heap are given to the priests, and the rejected material at the bottom to the Holeya. The hierarchical theme recurs in almost every context of life. On festive occasions, the Washerman, the Barikar, the Talawar, the Korava and the Holeya are given alms in that order.

The social map of Shivapur would be somewhat misleading if we failed to mention the links with other villages. There is a clear existence of inter-village connections. The caste and sub-caste affiliations cut across the territorial boundaries of the village. A caste or a sub-caste member has relations with men of the same caste or sub-caste outside the village. This is a horizontal spread which is reflected in the interrelationships between Shivapur and the neighbouring, and occasionally with distant, villages. Such interrelationships are sustained by caste ties, feelings and sentiments. Shivapur has such links with about nine villages in the vicinity. Religion is another factor which has created such inter-village contacts. The Muslims of Shivapur often take

their disputes for settlement to Hubli or Dharwar where
they have fellow-Muslims in whom they repose trust. The
high priests of the Lingayats, Marathas, Jains and Brahmans
who live outside the village claim extra-territorial loyalties.
For instance, some high priests of the Lingayat caste live
beyond even the district of Dhawar, and the Lingayats of
Shivapur often undertake long journeys to these centres for
religious purposes. The occupational specialists—the priest,
the carpenter, the goldsmith and the blacksmith—serve the
neighbouring village as well. The local goldsmith, the blacksmith and the carpenter are known for their skill. The blacksmith of Shivapur, Ningappa, is said to be in great demand
in the local market and neighbouring villages. These
economic relationships have drawn the outsiders into the
local life. There are also interests arising out of common
borders. The boundaries of the neighbouring villages inter-
sect at Shivapur, and in consequence common land interests
between them have arisen. The marital ties form another
network of inter-village relationships. Religious festivals are
organised in co-operation with neighbouring villages since
they involve a large amount of money. The festival of
Dyamavva, recently celebrated in Shivapur, is a case in point.
The people of Shivapur collected funds from neighbouring
villages, which came forth with their contributions on condition that the festival should be celebrated in turns in these
villages.

III

AYA AND THE CASTE

I

THE *AYA* SYSTEM as it operates in Shivapur is a well-organised institution. As such, its institutional functions and relationships form part of the larger and total complex of social institutions of the village. In particular, basic links have been forged between the caste system and the *Aya* system. In point of fact, the caste system has links with every institution in the village since it is the pivot on which the community life turns. It is these links which constitute the ultimate stabilising factors of Shivapur society. The *Aya* system has links not only with caste, but with other institutions as well. Here we shall focus our attention on the relationship between the *Aya* and the caste, always keeping in mind the fundamental axiom that a society is a totality and functions only as a whole. The study of the relationship between caste and the *Aya* system amounts to a study of the economic aspect of caste.

Megasthenes, a Greek traveller, who was around in India during the 4th century B.C., was the first writer to refer to the caste system, and it is interesting that he notes the complexity of the system. He refers to its occupational basis and to endogamy as its important characteristics. Later on caste has been the subject of casual observation or systematic study by traders, travellers and social scientists. Apparently the economic aspect of caste was first studied by W. H. Wiser, a Christian missionary, in the 1930's. His observations were based on his study of a village in the then United

Provinces. His approach to caste was exclusively economic. According to him, the artisan and the servile castes usually served the dominant caste. In short, he tended to look at the institution as primarily a means of economic exploitation. Since the economy was a subsistent one, social mobility was minimal. This narrow and uni-casual perspective made Wiser's analysis over-simple and his model of the caste system distorted. Among most recent studies we have Beidelman's 'Comparative Study of the Jajmani System' as a whole (1963), and this, too, emphasises the economic factor as the determinant of social processes. In our study we propose to depart from such an approach, and take a totalistic approach. If one looks at caste this way, one would see the current situation in the village as a complex pattern of relationships between tradition and change.

In the caste system, especially, such a total approach is essential since it is a system embracing more than merely economic relationships. The caste of an individual is determined by birth, and, once caste is determined, virtually everything about him—his occupation and the whole complex of his behaviour patterns and values—is determined. That is why it should be emphasised that the individual's occupation must not be viewed solely as an economic institution. For instance, it is pretty clear that change of one's occupation is not permitted by custom and is further limited by the severe lack of local opportunities. Since caste determines occupations, it is not correct to describe occupation as a merely economic institution.

The *Aya* system has to be fitted into the total social pattern, and the greatest danger here is to look at this institution in terms of the modern atomistic, cash-oiled economic machinery. The *Aya* system involves a series of economic transactions between a farmer and farmer, farmer and non-farmer, non-farmer and non-farmer, and between other groups. An important point to note about these transactions is that they present a variety of relationships. They are believed to be of mutual benefit, and both parties are governed by such a belief. They involve economic and social relations of give-and-take. The totality of these transactions is structured as an institution.

What are the factors that have given rise to the *Aya* system? It is centred around the values of honour, pride and prestige, and these values are further crystallised around the land in Shivapur. In consequence the *Aya* institution may be said to have arisen to give institutional expression to these values. It is characterised by the qualities of reciprocity and redistribution, harmony and co-operation. One of the easiest and commonest mistakes in studying it is to equate it with a system of inequality. The essence of the *Aya* system is that it obliterates the dichotomy between master and servant. It is based on the principle which we, from a modern angle, would call the reversibility of the master-servant paradigm. This means that a master feels as much dependent on the servant as the latter does on the former, and each has his own prestige which the other can upset byond a certain limit only at a risk. In Shivapur, for instance, the donor/donee distinction is blurred. The parties are respectively known as the *Ayadakula* (the family giving *Aya*), and the *Ayagara* (the recipient of *Aya*). The customary *Aya* is always paid in kind, but other payments for services given outside the *Aya* system may be made in cash.

Since the occupations are graded into a hierarchy of their own, with purity and pollution rules affecting relations with other occupations, and since the occupations are born into via the institution of caste, the question of higher and lower in a simple form does not arise. You are just where you are, and there is no external standard by which you can feel the sense of 'lower' and 'higher'. It is of the utmost importance that one should not overemphasise the economic aspect of the situation. Equally, to view the power relationship in terms of controller/controlled is also misleading. The central principle here is the *Dharma* or 'Duty'. All the parties are equalised as persons with duties. These duties should be performed without any grumbling. The client/tenant notion is completely foreign to the spirit of the *Aya* system. Who gives and who takes is a matter of shifting perspectives and contexts. The duties of each are fixed by birth, but the determination of who gives and who takes is not.

In the Wiser study there are 24 *Ayagaras,* whereas in Shivapur we encounter only 9 strict *Ayagaras.* The priest and the farmer are not *Ayagaras.* The farmer is the *Ayadakula,* but the priest is neither *Ayagara* nor *Ayadakula.* In Shivapur the *Ayagaras* are the Hadapad (barber), the Badiga (carpenter), the Kambar (blacksmith), the Agasa (washerman), the Barikar (village servant/labourer), the Talawar (village servant-land labourer/basket-maker), the Korava (instrumental musician), the Cheluvadi (the untouchable servant) and the Madiga (the untouchable labourer/leather-worker). Of these the barber and one of the two blacksmiths belong to the high-caste of Lingayat, and the washerman is a Muslim. One important fact which dispels the image of the *Aya* is that the artisans do not depend totally on the farmer. Their services are linked with the moral notion of *Dharma.* It is performed in obedience to the demands of one's *Dharma.* They also have a secondary occupation, and for these non-traditional services they are paid extra and in cash. The *Aya* system is a complex institution with economic, religious, moral and social functions.

Economically the *Ayagaras* contribute to the working of the agricultural economy. They provide the technological apparatus required by the local economy. The *Aya* has a religious aspect in so far as it is associated with purity and pollution rules. Its moral aspect concerns the fact that it is supposed to sustain the ideal of *Dharma.* Its social aspect concerns the fact that the system contributes to the successful performance of village festivals and other communal activities. On such occasions each *Ayagara* is expected to do his bit. An interesting religious context wherein an *Ayagara* plays an important role is during the ceremony in which a person who has taken a vow to propitiate the local god Basava fulfils that vow. During this ceremony the person who has taken the vow is expected to walk on a path covered with cloth to the Basava temple. The washerman, an *Aya-gara*, is the one who spreads such cloth.

The reason why the *Aya* system cannot be reduced to a simple matter of economics is that it is an intricately balanced pattern of economic and other elements. The economic motives behind the system are perfectly compatible with the social and moral goals, and this makes for the balance. The economic need for specialisation of the artisans is articulated with the social system, especially its central principle, that of caste. The system does not lead to any economic exploitation because there is a profoundly personal element in it. This element acts as a bulwark against any possible injustice by any of the parties involved in it. Of course, the prevalence of the ideal of the *Dharma* is an important factor which further insures against such an eventuality. All this may be explained by the fact that the economy is a closed one, based, not on cash dealing, but on an exchange of gifts. In such a system, naturally, there are no organised corporate activities such as are undertaken by trade unions. The degree of participation by the various parties is limited, and values are emphasised more than goods. The system presupposes a complex arrangement of transactions. Its main motto is *'Give more, Receive less'*. If all concerned follow this ideal, there can be no injustice.

We are now in a position to provide a clearer account of the basic features of the *Aya* system. First of all, it is held together by customary rules enforced by the agency of customary authorities. Secondly, it is built on the firm foundation of common interests and forces. This is evident during periods of both crisis and prosperity. If a crisis occurs, the *Ayagaras* come forward with free services. If there is a period of more than normal prosperity, the *Aya-dakulas* do not hesitate to give more than is traditionally required. Thirdly, the system reveals a nicely adjusted configuration of several parts into a whole. There is interdependence all along its main lines, and all this leads to automatic adjustment of part to part. Thus the whole mechanism operates as a single totality. Fourthly, it must be admitted that the system has its inadequacies, and these, too, become manifest during the periods of crisis and prosperity. All persons are not helped during a crisis, and during a prosperous period wide disparities may exist with regard to the proportion between giving and receiving. But at the same time it should be noted that such imbalance and mal-adjustment are not normal features, and they represent clear deviation from the accepted patterns.

The system is not based on any egalitarian ideology of the modern type. Rather is it based on the idea that each has a role to play in the drama of the community life as a whole. Each role is not a simple one, but a complex one, consisting of economic, moral and social functions. In the last analysis, the balance of the system is maintained by the fact that when power of one kind, like economic, tends to dominate, other kinds of power, religious or social, are automatically gener-ated to counteract it.

2

In a Shivapur village the social system as a whole is reflected in the *Aya* system. This means, of course, that the caste system as such is not reflected in the *Aya* system, but is in fact the central pillar of the system. We have seen from the caste map of Shivapur that the priestly function is performed by the sub-castes of the Lingayats down to and including the Pujar sub-caste. The person who performs the priestly func-tions is not technically an *Ayagara*, since payment is made to him ritualistically, and not for any services similar to those offered by the *Ayagaras*. The untouchables (*Holeya*) are not recognised for religious purposes by the priests of the other high-castes, though the untouchables themselves practise the Hindu rituals and participate in the economic system. In other words, they are *excluded religiously* but *included economic-ally*. Within priestly sub-castes, there are other shades of distinction.

Aya *and the Caste*

The two major priestly groups are the Hiremath and the Chikkamath among the Lingayats. As we have already had occasion to observe, the Brahman's role in Shivapur is negligible, for all practical purposes. The other priestly groups, after the Hiremath and the Chikkamath, may be called the minor priestly groups. While the payment is sent to the first two priestly groups, the minor priestly groups, though not *Ayagaras*, will have to go to the homes of the people, like the *Ayagaras*, for their collections. The goldsmith, though an artisan, is not strictly an *Ayagara*. He is charged with the magical function of making bracelets and amulets, believed to ward off evils or to bring about desirable states of affairs, like fertility. The goldsmith also performs ritualistic duties such as ear-boring. It is true that he is paid for his services as a goldsmith simply. But for his magico-religious functions he gets a special kind of payment which is recognised as such by being given a special name. This is the *Ulipi*, which should not be confused with the *Aya*. The *Ulipi* gives a ritual status.

The reason we propose to exclude the goldsmith from the list of the *Ayagaras* is that his services and payment are not related to the land economy as such, whereas, as we have been pointing out, the *Aya* system, so far as its economic aspect goes, is related to the land economy. His economic role, and he certainly has one, is not part of the land economy, but is related to the modern cash economy. Thus he exemplifies most dramatically the dual nature of the Shivapur economy. The goldsmith's role is both complex and fascinating. In the first place, he has a ritualistic, magical and religious function. In the second place, he has an economic function unrelated to the *Aya* system. In our view most studies of Indian villages have failed to come to grips with the dualistic and ambiguous nature of the goldsmith's role in the village community. At the same time one ought not to jump to the conclusion that the goldsmith is a sort of priest. Such misleading simplifications can be avoided if one pays proper attention to the language of the village.

Aya *and the* Caste

In Shivapur the people make a clear distinction between three kinds of gifts—the *Kanike*, the *Aya* and the *Ulipi*. What is given to the priest is called the *Kanike*; what is given to the *Ayagaras* for their economic services is called *Aya*; and what is given to the goldsmith for his magico-religious services is called *Ulipi*. This distinction is clearly meant to suggest that the goldsmith is neither an *Ayagara* nor a priest. Even within the *Aya* pattern there are complications. The *Ayagaras* have primary occupations, and these come within the *Aya* system proper. But most *Ayagaras* also have secondary or tertiary occupations which remain outside the Shivapur view of the *Aya* system. Only the goldsmith, the carpenter (excepting one), the washerman, the blacksmith, the Barikar, the Talawar, the Korava and the Holeya are generally landless. But even so they work as labourers. Thus one has to accept the idea that the *Aya* system, while being central to the economy of the village, does not comprehend the sum total of economic activities. Shivapur may be said to operate with a dual economy, one related to the traditional *Aya* system, the other to the modern cash system.

The socio-economic ranking is related to the *Aya* system. Like the social system, the *Aya* system is also hierarchical. The hierarchical principle applies to the priestly group as well. One notices most vividly the articulation of the hierarchy during the *Aya* collection. There is a certain manner and order in which the collections are expected to be made. During the harvest, for instance, the best and topmost layers of the grain-heap are offered to the priestly castes in the order of the priestly hierarchy. Then follow the processions in the specific order, with the untouchable last. Among the priestly classes, all excepting the Hiremath and the Chikkamath go to collect their share. Even the Brahman and the Muslim priest go. The carpenter, the blacksmith and the washerman may or may not go. The lower caste group like the Barikar, the Talawar, the Korava, the Cheluvadi and the Madiga are expected to go and collect. However, there is also the personal factor which determines who may or may

43

not have the privilege of not going and yet getting the share directed to their homes. The same hierarchical pattern of procession obtains during ceremonies when food is given. The general principle seems to be that the lower the occupation, the greater the danger of pollution. But this intricate interdependent system is believed to derive its ultimate rationale and sanction from the *Dharma*.

At the same time we have noticed that socio-economic ranking is not necessarily high, as has been maintained with regard to this system as it operates in Northern India. The *Aya* is not solely socio-economic or religious. We also feel that the power relationship concept leading to the accusation of economic exploitation (see Beidelman as a spokesman of the group) is an over-simplification. The *Ayagara* has as much prestige as the *Ayadakula*. We have come across a number of cases in which the power of the *Ayagara* has matched the power of the *Ayadakula*. One interesting example may suffice. A carpenter in Shivapur voted against a Lingayat farmer during the recent Panchayat elections. Now as is clear, the carpenter is an *Ayagara* and the farmer an *Ayadakula*. When the farmer attempted to intimidate him, the carpenter, in all dignity, refused to collect the *Aya* from his *Ayadakula*. Here we may see how simplified is the idea of economic exploitation. The economic and the ritual statuses are not correlated. A man may enjoy high status on ritualistic ground while economically he may be much lower. We would suggest it is again an over-simplification to consider inequality as the basic principle of the system. In fact, both the notions of equality and inequality seem to us equally important for a true understanding of the system.

The inequality idea is further weakened by the fact that the village society is a highly kin-oriented one, and that this would cut across economic status. While it is true that hierarchy is a principle which cannot be completely divorced from the idea of inequality, it is no less true that in Shivapur there exists factors and forces which tend to effect such a dissociation. In so far as they exist, inequality is not an actuality.

44

Aya *and the Caste*

We have to go back to our idea of dualism. The key to any understanding of Shivapur today is this idea. Inequality may be said to exist, but so also equality. It is, in consequence, as grave an error to call the system egalitarian as it is to accuse it of being based solely on inequality.

3

The economic system of Shivapur is predominantly agricultural, but it has its non-agricultural components as well. Most caste groups below the Muslim are practically landless, and they constitute a little more than 50 per cent of the village population. Thus agriculture is not the only means of livelihood for the villagers. Those who are without land become labourers. In consequence one may conceive of two complementary systems of land and labour. The *Aya* system is based on the principle of equality of exchange. The assumption is that when a transaction occurs, both the parties give. The equality between the parties refers to, not the quantum of gift, but simply the fact of gift. Hence the *Aya* economy is sustained by the institution of caste.

Occupational specialisation leads to caste, and eventually this leads to an intricate and inevitable network of interdependence. Everyone is necessarily specialised, and this means that none can do without the others. Here there are no modern agencies like the hospital or the social services. There are no educational institutions, excepting the traditional ones. Not only do such agencies not exist, but—and this is the main point—the attitudes and habits of behaviour which sustain such agencies do not exist either. For instance, modern-type educational institutions, even if established, would fail to function since there exists no sustaining pattern of attitudes and behaviour. The fact of interdependence can hardly be exaggerated.

In the urban areas, if one barber is found unsatisfactory, you can go to another. In the village such a choice does not exist. One must visit the traditional barber. There are stories of how members of the high castes were forced to seek the services of the artisans whom they had initially antagonised. This is, after all, a small, face-to-face community in which everybody knows everybody else. In such a community interdependence is inevitable. The farmers belong to a particular caste, and the non-farmers to other castes. The economy is a self-sufficient but minimal one. There are hardly ten families which are not heavily indebted. Among the non-farmers, we have both the artisans and the labourers. The pattern of mutual obligations and dependence is strongly reinforced by the nature of the agrarian calendar. The farmer needs the services of the artisans or the priests as badly as the latter needs the services of the former. The whole agricultural process involves the co-operation of virtually all the other castes at different stages.

The priest, who is a ritual dignitary, mediates between man and God. His special status is related to the fact that he can propitiate the great powers beyond. The people of Shivapur have a deep-rooted habit of locating the causes of their illnesses, misfortunes such as bad health, and good events, in the supernatural realm. The priest is the man who can establish effective liaison between the visible and the invisible, the human and the divine. This accounts for the dependence of the village on the priest.

In a sense each occupation and each caste-sub/caste is a monopoly, because no one can compete with them, *within the local system*, for the functions they perform. This is, in fact, their strength, and this is also the reason why the system has a series of effective internal balances. Even the untouchable is absolutely necessary for the kind of services he alone can render. There are intimate and necessary relationships, not only between farmer and non-farmer, but also between non-farmer and non-farmer. The barber depends upon the carpenter as much as the farmer does on both. In this connection an interesting incident which took place recently may be cited. A barber had newly arrived in the village as an immigrant, and naturally he was in bad need of local support. To win local custom he was only too eager to offer his services. The local carpenter sensed the situation and turned this to his advantage. He helped him freely in the building of his house. The barber, in return, offered to serve the carpenter for life without any charge for his services. Not only this, the carpenter is often given extra treatment by the barber, which makes him feel happy.

This is not a cash economy since no one works exclusively for money. Yet, as already hinted, this is a dual economy in which there are transactions which can only be explained as belonging to a cash economy. It is significant that persons with motives of making money go out of the village, since the Shivapur economy discourages such efforts. Four of the local washermen, eager to make money, had to open their centre of business in Dharwar, while keeping to their traditional job in the village. The basic principle of interdependence limits the possiblities of cash economy in the village life.

While admitting economic activities which may fall outside the scope of the *Aya* system, we may assert that every individual and caste is drawn into the *Aya* system in one context or another. The caste, of course, is the key institution here as in every other aspect of Shivapur life. It is this institution which structurally knits together the various threads of Shivapur social life. But then, one may ask, how is caste supported? The answer would be by the whole of society with its myriad institutions and their operations. Caste sustains the social fabric as much as the social fabric sustains the caste. In fact, the two can be separated only for purposes of study, and, *in terms of living processes*, it is absurd to draw such distinctions. The same social mechanisms which keep the social life of Shivapur going are the ones that sustain and facilitate the working of the *Aya* system. Of these, the most important are the street/caste/village councils and the customary/positive law.

Society is, from a broader perspective, made up of similar and dissimilar interests. Similar interests are as much connected as dissimilar ones. The similar interests may crystallise into caste or sub-caste groups, but a series of dissimilar and disconnected interests cannot lead to social existence. Links have to be provided between these dissimilar interests. Such links, paradoxically, arise because there are similar interests between dissimilar interest groups. This is the ultimate principle of social existence. In Shivapur, too, this is the case. Members of the same caste obviously have similar interests and hence they form into organised groups. But members of one caste depend, for one purpose or another, on other castes/sub-castes. This interdependence is of the very texture of Shivapur's social fabric.

In Shivapur, each caste or sub-caste or occupational group functions in such a total way that one can speak of each as a way of living. Thus Shivapur is a system of many ways of life, but all converging at innumerable points frequently enough to constitute a common way of life. The basic mores that support this system are characteristically dualistic. They are at the same time equal relationships and hierarchical relationships. These may be regarded as horizontal and vertical relationships. The kinship relations, for example, belong to the horizontal line, whereas the caste system as a whole belongs to the vertical line. They are all governed by the basic moral injunctions of the society, like 'It is good to protect one. It is good to give more, not less.'

Such a complicated machinery cannot work without some all-pervasive belief or spirit. This belief that animates the system as a whole is the belief that the system is good because it has been proved to be good. Otherwise, how did their ancestors accept it and hand it on to them? This belief is also pragmatically supported by the fact that the system leads to mutual benefit and hence must be good. There is, undoubtedly, the belief in *Dharma*, which has been an important element in regulating social as well as individual behaviour. All the participants in the *Aya* system are unconsciously governed by the notion that it is their *Dharma* to do thus and thus, and not otherwise. *Dharma*, a key

Aya *and the Caste*

notion in Hindu life and thought, may be translated broadly as 'duty' and perhaps more accurately as 'the law of one's essential being'.

Lastly, we may take note of the interesting and important fact that there exists in Shivapur, not only caste differentiation, but *Aya* differentiation. We have already noticed in another context the distinction between *Kanike, Ulipi* and *Aya*. The *Aya* differentiation is reflected in the different terms employed to designate the payments made to different parties. The word 'Aya' is not used in all cases, and we have used it only for the purpose of designating the system as a whole. It is therefore necessary to remember that the people themselves do not use the term 'Aya' in this blanket sense, and that they use a number of terms to indicate different levels of *Aya*. The caste differentiation is paralleled not only in this *Aya* system; it is also clearly continued in the village pantheon. The village duties are also hierarchically arranged. Those belonging to the higher castes are assigned higher status, and those belonging to the Holeyas the lowest status. Thus there is a recurrent theme and pattern at different levels and in different areas. This constant interaction upholds the unity and totality of the Shivapur social system.

IV

RIGHTS AND RESPONSIBILITIES

I

WE SHALL NOW attempt a descriptive account of the rights and responsibilities implied and generally accepted in the working of the *Aya* system in Shivapur. As already indicated, there is a close identification of occupation with caste and sub-caste. Whenever a family is forced to take an occupation which does not traditionally belong to it, it tends to become endogamic and crystallise itself into a new sub-caste around the new occupation. In Shivapur the Lingayat family which has turned to the occupation of blacksmith illustrates this process. Now this family has forged out a sub-caste of its own. Caste/sub-caste imply rights and responsibilities both functionally and socially, and these are at the very heart of the dynamics of the *Aya* system.

If we may make a generalisation, the self-sufficiency of a village in functional terms is never complete. Generally no village community has within its territorial limits all the functional groups necessary to the continuance of social existence. For instance, the Wiser study lists only 24 functions, and in Shivapur there are not even half that number. In consequence the deficiency has to be made good, and this is effected through the visit of the necessary functionaries from the neighbouring villages or even far-off places. The village society is made to develop affiliations economically, even ritualistically, with the outside world. Equally, Shivapur itself is able to make good the deficiencies of neighbouring villages. For instance, the priests, the artisans and the washermen of Shivapur cater to the needs of some of the neighbouring villages as well.

Before giving a systematic account of the functional groups in the village, we may first introduce those functionaries who are outsiders normally but whom Shivapur has drawn into the pattern of its existence from necessity. We shall take the potter first. Shivapur has no potter of its own, and this is a rather serious deficiency in view of the importance of pottery both secularly and ritualistically in the life of the village. Pots, of course, are necessary for some of the important routine requirements of living. They are necessary in the processes of cooking, carrying water and the storing of goods. Pots are essential also in important rituals. In the marriage ceremony, for instance, there is a practice of keeping five pots at the five corners of the ceremonial platform on which the bride and bridegroom are seated while undergoing the ceremony. The five pots are linked by a thread. Shivapur depends for its supply of pottery on outside talents whom we may call the guest functionaries. There are three potters, one each from Garag, Hebballi and Dharwar, who serve the Shivapur inhabitants. All these places are within a radius of about 12 miles.

It is interesting that a distinction is made with regard to the services required for material and ritualistic purposes. So far as the material need is concerned, potters from Garag and Hebballi visit the village once a year, and sell their goods both for cash and kind. Sometimes when they are not immediately paid for their goods. they have to return during the harvest season when the villagers are naturally in a better position to pay. As a result, the economic relations tend to become more than casual, and the links of the visiting functionaries with Shivapur more regular. The visiting potter camps at the village tank and within the neighbourhood of the Lingayats, but not the visiting brass-worker, who is a Muslim, and hence of a lower caste status. The latter camps near the local mosque. For the religious requirements of marriage, pottery is usually brought from Dharwar.

51

The pot is brought into the village ceremoniously. It is first kept either with a kinsman or with someone belonging to the same caste and then taken into the house in a procession.

The village now lacks its own oil-presser. Formerly there used to be a Lingayat family which specialised in the occupation, but it now no longer performs this function. There also used to be a Rajaput doing it, but he also has retired after serving Shivapur for 25 years. Hence it is necessary to seek external service. The local oil-presser is now being replaced by the 'Grammodyoga' centre, an urban-oriented and goal-directed unit under the State policy of helping the village economy, at Dharwar. The village is without brass-workers. A brass-worker from the coastal area about 50 miles away visits the village once a year. There is no fixed time when he is expected to come, but usually it is round about October. The village also depends upon the services of masons (*Uppar*) who come from the neighbouring villages of Sattur and Amaragol, and the bigger town of Dharwar.

We shall postpone a group-by-group description of the functions to a later stage and confine ourselves to the general system of rights and responsibilities, which supports the *Aya* system. To the questions 'why do these functional groups perform their services? How is the social system actually sustained?', the answer clearly lies in the system of rights and responsibilities. However, it has to be noted that the network of relationships is not simply confined to those between the artisan and non-artisan. It is more comprehensive and includes such relationships as those between the landowner and the landless, the ritual dignitaries and the rest of the community, the high-caste and the low-caste, men and women, and the rich and the poor. The sum total of all these relations constitutes the *Aya* system of Shivapur. There is differentiation socially on the basis of caste, and the *Jita* system is differentiated on the same basis.

A preliminary distinction between the *Aya* and the *Jita* is necessary before the *Aya* is examined in detail. The *Jita* is explicitly a contractual payment. It involves the payment of a fixed sum of money within a specified time-limit. It is generally a relationship involving one's own castemen, but not always. But if the *Jita* relation involves one's own caste-man, the *Jitagara* is allowed to eat with the family and live as one of the household. In sharp contrast, the *Aya* involves necessarily a member of a different caste or sub-caste. It is liable to be withdrawn since it is not contractual like the *Jita*. The *Aya* is associated with privilege, prestige and honour, whereas the *Jita* is a matter of simple economic necessity. The *Jita* is impersonal since it is contractual, and it is not reciprocal in the sense in which *Aya* is. In Shivapur the *Aya* partakes at the same time of the nature of both a gift and a service, both given and received. In fact, in a subtle manner it obliterates the distinction between the giver and the receiver. It is a comprehensive term which includes moral, economic, religious and social elements. It is obligatory and customary. It is morally and religiously sanctioned by the *Dharma*. Here a warning must be given against attempts to regard the *Aya* as a merely economic relationship. Moreover, the *Aya* is not the only kind of economic relationship in the village. There are others like the *Jita*, the *Vata*, the *Vatti* or the *Kaigada*.

In the *Vata* transaction, one borrows grain and promises to return it in kind or cash after the lapse of a fixed time; the *Vatti* is a mortgage transaction with a time limit. The *Kaigada* is in the nature of a loan, to be repaid with or without interest.

The *Aya* has both a sacred and a secular aspect, and this becomes evident if one examines the system in its entire complexity. There are eleven distinct kinds of gift-payments associated with the system, and each is given a separate name. We shall now see what these gifts are, and what is their purpose.

1 *Dakshine*. This is a purely religious payment made of ritualistic services, in addition to the food and clothing

offered to the priest. The *Dakshine* amount is in fives or multiples of five. It starts from 5 Paise and normally goes up to 5 Rupees.

2 *Bhiksha*. This is given to a lesser religious dignitary, and it may also be given to a mendicant.

3 *Ulipi*. This is a general sort of a gift to all religious dignitaries or to persons who are not religious functionaries but who may be offering religious services. The artisans, for example, are given *Ulipi* when they render a ritualistic service, as in the case of the goldsmith. This is to be taken as an extra gift paid to the artisans in addition to the payment made for their occupational services. *Ulipi* is given in the form of an assortment of bananas, dry dates, dry grapes, coconuts, rice or pulses.

4 *Kushi*. This is given only to the lower castes from the Barikar downwards, during festive and religious occasions. It is an extra gift, given out of sheer joy produced by the occasion. The word 'kushi' means joy.

5 *Bab*. This is paid to individuals as well as to institutions or groups and is a rather frequently made payment. All the dozen gods and goddesses of the village are paid *Bab* at engagements and marriages. At the time of division of the ancestral family it is given in the form of money to certain temples as a matter of custom. As a rule, money given as *Bab* goes to the temple. If it is in the form of food, it goes to the worshipper. When *Bab* is rendered to the Basava temple on the hill, the Mathapati gets the food, and the money part of it goes to the temple fund. During the harvest time, custom requires that the owners of the 'lower fields' pay *Bab* to the hill Basava temple. The owners of the Dandinadari ('the way the army went') fields are expected to give *Bab* to the Hugar during the harvest time. Those from Sulla village give *Bab* to the Pujar during the harvest time. Also eligible for *Bab* are all priests, whether Lingayat, Maratha or Muslim, and all other ritual dignitaries of all castes, as well as the Korava (the instrumental musician) and the Kuruba who plays the drum during temple festivals. The

Rights and Responsibilities

Bab is paid as a gesture of gratitude to God and His man, the priest, for their blessings.

6 *Nidhi.* This is given in the form of grain. The practice in the village is that the harvested grain is taken ceremoniously through the village. All the temples on the way are given their *Nidhi* in the form of a basketful of the new grain. The grain thus offered is shared by the temple as well as the worshipper. It is given by the land-owning class during harvests, and all, including the landless, give both *Nidhi* and *Bab* during festive and ceremonial occasions.

7 *Aya* proper. This is paid in accordance with one's status in the social and occupational scale, and with one's caste status as well. The status of both the giver and the receiver is taken into account. This is not a measured gift, the donor being merely expected to give it. The idea is that it is better to give more than less.

8 *Susaya.* This gift is, in a sense, measured out. The practice is that grains must be given in such a way that they overflow a given container, which could be a basket, bag, etc. Even fodder is also given as *Susaya.* It is usually given by a big farmer, and the giver of *Susaya* ranks next to the one who gives the *Aya.* This is on the assumption that to give a measured quantity is a lesser act than giving without limit.

9 *Alategalu*, which may be translated as 'measured grain'. The quantum of payment here is more precisely measured out.

10 *Tundaya.* This is also measured out, but the emphasis is on fragmentation, not on the measured limit itself. The word 'Tundu' means a fragment. Like the measured variety, this also is not considered generous.

11 *Holeaya.* This is the reject left over at the harvest heap after the *Aya* has been distributed hierarchically, beginning with the priest. It may also be the grain which clings to the fringes of the harvest pit after it has been emptied or which may remain as left-over at the bottom of the pit. It is also applied to the material put in the winnowing basket of

bamboo at the time of death. It usually consists of chillies, grain, salt, etc., meant for the dead one on his or her journey. All these are given to the untouchable (*Holeya*). He is the one who is expected to do the dirty and risky job of digging the harvest pit or cleaning it, or digging the grave. It is significant that these payments are hierarchically arranged, with the one to the priest at the top and the one to the untouchable at the bottom. This hierarchical pattern is repeated everywhere.

2

We are now equipped with a general perspective of the whole *Aya* system, and we may proceed to take up the occupations one by one.

The Priest: The Brahman, Lingayat, and Muslim castes alone have priests, who are called *Bhat, Jangam* and *Mulla* respectively. The lower caste groups have their Brahman or Lingayat priest according to their shifting needs. There are 3 Brahman, 3 Lingayat, 2 Muslim and one Maratha households of priests in the village. Of these the Maratha priest does not belong to the priestly caste by birth. He has acquired priesthood subsequently and has been raised to the status of priest (*Sant*). The Rajaputs have a man who is consulted for the ritual calendar, but he is not a full-fledged priest. Each of these priests is considered essential to his respective caste group, and has also made himself indispensable to the lower castes.

The role of the priest may be seen from two points of view. First, there is his role in the life-career of the individual, from birth to death. Then there is his role in respect to the rituals and ceremonies of the group. The life of the individual in Shivapur is regulated by a series of sacraments performed at crucial stages of his life, each signalling the entry into a new stage. At the time of birth, the priest is necessary to bless the new-born with his religious incantations (*Mantra*). Then he is again needed for the naming and tonsure ceremonies. The puberty rites of a girl, her marriage ceremony, the consummation ceremony, the time of pregnancy and the death ceremony, all require the priest and his religious services. During these ceremonies, the ritual status of the individual undergoes a change, and the priest assists him, prescribing the holy bath and chanting the sacred 'Mantras'. The person concerned invariably resorts to the purificatory, ritual bath at these times. After tonsure, puberty or death, he is supposed to be polluted, and, in consequence, he has to take a ritual bath in order to be restored to his normal status. The priest's role in the life of the family is quite important. When a new house is built, there is the ceremony of first entry into it. This involves a ritual act at which the priest officiates. During the family festivals, he is required to offer worship to the gods in the home. He is also consulted when buying new land, and the newly bought land has to be consecrated by his rites. He also must bless the newly purchased cattle.

There are certain festivals which involve the members of the caste as a whole, and on these occasions the priest's services are naturally indispensable. There are inter-religious occasions in which the village as a whole participates. On such occasions a priest is honoured as a priest, not as one belonging to this or that caste/religious group. At such times the presence of all the priests is welcomed, and they are given gifts. It may be observed that an inter-religious occasion is not necessarily one involving the whole village. It may also arise in the life of an individual or family. The priest also has an important function in preserving the folklore, the folk culture and the folk religion. He is an embodiment of these values. He recites religious texts like the *Puranas*, the *Punyakathas*, the *Koran*, etc. His rights are fundamentally linked with his duties and responsibilities. The gifts he receives such as the *Kanike, Dakshine, Bhiksha, Ulipi, Bab and Nidhi* are given as of right, in recognition of his functions and responsibilities. The seasonal gifts with which he is showered are geared to the economic calendar. One could even suggest that the gift-calendar and the agrarian calendar are perfectly correlated. During August, September, October, March and April, when important festivals are observed, the priests are given seasonal gifts such as coconuts, sweets, etc. They are offered *Kartika Bhiksha* in the form of grains during the *Deepavali*, the festival of lights. On New Year's day *Ugadi* grain is offered as a gift. During the various seasons, either the farmers send the gifts to the priests or the priests approach them for gifts. The nature of a gift is related to the event which occasions it.

The gifts may take five forms, namely a cow, gold, land, cloth and grain, in that order of importance. The highest gift is the gift of a cow (*Godana*). The birth of a first son or the birth of a child in old age may be considered an important enough event to prompt the gift of a cow to the priest. When a child is born under an inauspicious star, like the Mula Star (*Mula Nakshatra*), there is a special rite by which the evil influence is eliminated. A basket tray loaded with grain, cloth, etc., along with the child is waved across the cow's face. Later on everything, the basket, the cow, etc., except the child, is given to the priest who officiates at the rite. The idea is that with the gift go the sins. The priest is both purifier and the carrier of sins. At the time of death, too, a cow-gift may be given. With this, among the Lingayats a ceremony called *vibhuti vile* is associated. After offering this gift, if a person survives he is considered a sinful man. His sight is avoided in the earlier part of the day as an evil influence. The gifts offered at the time of death reflect the age, status and value of the dead man.

A cow-gift is regarded as a prestige gift. Recently, at Shivapur the death of an old man was marked by a cow-gift. If a girl menstruates for the first time on an inauspicious day, there has to be a special ceremony. Another ceremony, that of welcoming the dead occurs usually within the first fortnight after the day of death. In this connection it may be mentioned that all except the Brahmans, Jains, Marathas and Rajaputs, bury their dead. The ceremony of welcoming the dead involves the cult of ancestor worship. This may be most clearly seen in the fact that the dead elders form the core of the ancestors and join the ranks of the gods in heaven. Among the Lingayats a small vessel and the phallic symbol, representing the dead, are newly made and a ceremony is performed by the eldest son. At this ceremony the food dear to the departed person is cooked and offered. After this ceremony the dead achieve the status of a god. The priest declares:

'The dead man has become a god. Worship him from now as a god.''

These are all occasions which are punctuated with appropriate gifts to the lesser priests; among the Lingayats all priests excepting the ranks of the Hiremath and Chikkamath, and the Bawa among the Muslims, function as their professional assistants. Among the Lingayats, the Hugar fetches the flowers and the Mathapati sends out the invitation on these occasions. These lesser dignitaries worship the family gods at the request of the family on these occasions.

During the *Ramzan* time, the Muslim Bawa chants the sacred texts of the Koran at the break of dawn, alerting the believers about the holy season. The Maratha priest, the *sant,* announces the arrival of the festival of *Shivajayanti* and the *Dindi* festivals. Thus the lesser dignitaries of the priestly class keep the whole village informed of the religious and ritual calendar. The role of the priest of every rank and group is therefore related to the total pattern of social existence at Shivapur. Regarding the gifts there are standard expectations. Ideally one is expected to give 12 *Ulipis* at a marriage ceremony. Of these, 9 go to the village gods and 3 to the religious establishments (*Maths*). Also the Barikar and the village Headman expect to be given one each.

Then there is the payment made by the village community as a whole in the form of land. The Lingayat and the Muslim priests as well as the lesser religious dignitaries are granted a land-gift by the village. Land thus given away is the personal property of the religious dignitaries who receive it. In the assignment of ritual work, the higher priest is in charge of the higher rituals while the lesser one is entrusted with the lesser. It is the lesser dignitaries like the Hugar, the Ganachari, etc., who are charged with the responsibility of maintaining the village temples. They are expected to keep them clean, have them white-washed on festive occasions, bathe the gods on certain fixed days every week, and treat the gods to an oil-bath on special occasions. They are the ones to offer flowers to the gods and receive the food offering to the gods (*Yedi*) given by the devotees. As we have seen, the rituals are generally integrated into the system of land economy.

The *Artisan* (Panchal): We will examine the panchala's occupation by occupation, beginning with the goldsmith (*Pattar*). The name derives from the fact that he is one who can inspire *Pattu*, i.e., confidence or trust, in others. In the gold business it is so easy to cheat, and that may be the reason why so much importance is attached to the question of confidence. In Shivapur there are five goldsmith households. Two of them are local and the other three are immigrants from the coastal areas. As usual, the local goldsmith is considered superior in status to the immigrant. Further, they are divided into *Madi* (ritually pure) goldsmiths and the *Sada* (ordinary) goldsmiths. The *Madi* goldsmiths are naturally considered superior since they maintain more rigidly the ritual of purity. They bathe ritually and regularly, worship the anvil on which gold is beaten into the required shape and thinness, and do not prepare the magical objects like the amulets, the talismans, etc. They make pure ornaments whether related to aesthetic or religious values. These ornaments are those used for the ear-boring or nose-boring and wedding rings, and they may be ornaments of status value. The *Madi* goldsmith does not use coal, but charcoal. While fetching water or eating, he is a great purist. He wears little dress beyond the loin cloth. The *Sada* goldsmith is less pure ritualistically, wears more clothes, uses coal and makes magical objects like talismans.

The goldsmiths' main occupational work is to make gold ornaments, for the ears, nose, fingers, neck, arms, ankles, wrists, head, etc. It may be noted that these ornaments are related to the status of the wearers. They indicate the status of being a child, being in a post-puberty condition, being an adult, and being married. The responsibilities for getting the ornaments made are divided in accordance with the sex distinction. The father is responsible for a son's ornaments and the mother for a daughter's. The marital status or age of a woman can be determined by the ornaments she wears. For instance, old women do not wear nose ornaments. The unmarried girls cannot wear *Tali* (or the 'Mangala Sutra', the special necklace which the bridegroom ritualistically ties round her neck during the marriage). The married girls can be recognised by the innumerable ornaments with which they decorate their bodies from head to toe.

The economic and caste status of a woman can also be seen from her ornaments. A low-caste woman is not expected to wear certain ornaments like gold armlets (*Vanki*). She uses silver ornaments, whereas women of higher caste wear gold ones. The ornaments serve both aesthetic and ritualistic purposes. From birth to death, there are rites which involve the use of ornaments. Ornaments for the ears are necessary at the ear-boring ceremony, usually during the first, fifth or sixth month of the child's life. There is a belief associated with the ceremony. It is that, if the goldsmith bores the children's ears, scorpions and snakes will not bite them and they will not be afflicted with rickets.

The wedding ring is made of gold and there have to be two such rings, one given by the girl's parents and another by her husband's parents. In the *Tali* ceremony, which is part of the marriage, two 'Talis' of gold, one each from the parents of the bride and bridegroom, are required. They are sometimes made by one and the same goldsmith and sometimes not. These ritualistic ornaments are received from the goldsmith in a ceremonious manner. Five married women who are young and whose husbands are alive (*Muttaideyaru*) go to the goldsmith's house, carrying the *ulipi* presentation. They worship the goldsmith's fire-pot and the anvil. Then they give the goldsmith the present, burn incense, crack jokes, and perform *Arati* (a small vessel in which oil-soaked cottons wicks are lighted and waved up and down near the object which is supposed to be done *Arati*). Finally, they collect the ornaments and return home. Thus the occasion is a mixture of the moods of mirth and gravity.

The Brahmans are known as the *Dwija* or the twice-born, the ritualistic expression of which takes place once in boyhood and again at the time of marriage. The well-to-do try to show off their wealth by presenting the bridegroom with a gold sacred thread. The goldsmith who makes it is given presents, in addition to the payment for services. Nowadays, there is a very great demand on the goldsmith for making talismans and amulets, which are invested with magical properties. The payment for making them is nominal and symbolic, usually as small as 5 Paise. These are supposed to be made on those Sundays when there is an eclipse (solar or lunar) or on certain other auspicious days. They are meant to ward off evil spirits. They are expected to restore fertility or virility, and in general, bring the wearer good luck. Today, the goldsmith's popularity, if not the income, is largely due to his services as a maker of these magical objects. In Shivapur the goldsmith is attached to a family, since for generations a family will employ the services of the same family of goldsmiths. The goldsmith, as elsewhere elaborated, is not strictly an *Ayagara*.

The Carpenter (Badiga): There are 7 households of carpenters in Shivapur. Their occupation is to supply the *Ayada Kula* (farmer) with agricultural implements. The word '*kula*' means a plough. The quantity of grain due to them is fixed by the number of *kulas* owned by the farmers on whom they depend. This presentation is called *Alategalu* (measured grain). Each carpenter household depends upon from 20 to 50 households of farmers. Traditionally a carpenter has to make a set of implements for every plough or every pair of bullocks. These implements are hoe, plough, planter, reaper, harvester, etc. This set is made free as part of the *Aya* system. The services include the annual repairing of them in order to keep them fit for work. If necessary they must be replaced at the end of every three years. All other work above this is considered as extra, and for any extra work extra payment has to be made. The making of wheels for the bullock-cart, for instance, is extra work. So is the work done in house-building or the upkeep of the temples. Such work calls for separate payment. The low level of the village technology has naturally invested the carpenter with a ritual status. People talk of his *kaiguna* (the virtue inhering in the hand) as a mysterious quality.

The village goddess, Dyamavva, is a deity of the carpenters. The village has given 14 acres of land to the carpenters to attend to this goddess. She is a goddess of fertility. She is in special demand as the protectress of newly-wed girls. She is also considered effective against epidemics. She is believed to be the guardian of the lands. Before they start sowing, the farmers load the *Udi* (fold of the saree) of the goddess with gifts of coconut, banana, dry dates, etc. She is generally worshipped on all festive occasions. She is showered with gifts in the form of sarees, grain, ornaments and cash. Excepting the ornaments, all the other gifts offered to Dyamavva are distributed among the carpenters. There is here a fusion of ritual and economic status. Every plough or *kula* involves a presentation of a fixed quantity of grain.

The carpenters also receive other grain gifts throughout the year according to the agrarian calendar. During the sowing or harvesting season, for example, they get these gifts. During festivals, the carpenters do not go to collect food as a gift. As already mentioned, all carpenter families own temple land. Only one of them owns a personal holding of 28 acres of land. In this family, the eldest son and the one next to him have taken to the traditional occupation of carpentry, while the third and the youngest have turned into agriculturists. The carpenters also own cattle, mostly bullocks, and they collect gifts of fodder from farmers. They also collect fuel from them. On festive occasions they collect, in addition, grain, pulses and vegetables.

The Blacksmith (Kambar): There are 2 households, of which one practises carpentry as well. The family which does blacksmithing serves 50 *Ayadakulas*. The local black-smith is known for his skill, and his fame has travelled beyond Shivapur, so much so that he is called upon to serve several nearby villages. He is obliged to make certain objects under the traditional *Aya* system. These are agricultural implements like the sickle, the pickaxe, the axe, and a variety of hoes and sickles. The iron rim for the wheels of the bullock-cart is considered an extra and has to be paid for separately. His services in building a house or work in connection with temples are also considered extras, and call for extra payment.

As in the case of the carpenter, the blacksmith is given all sorts of gifts throughout the year. However, one of the blacksmiths who is a Lingayat does not go to collect food and extra grain. May and July, when there is sowing, August to October, when weddings normally take place, and January to March, when the harvest is collected, are busy months for the blacksmith as well as the carpenter. While the blacksmith is most busy during the months of August to October, the carpenter is busiest during the months of May to July. Both are equally busy during the harvest months, January to March. The one blacksmith who specialises exclusively in blacksmithing belongs to the Lin-gayat caste, whereas the other blacksmith who practises carpentry as well belongs to the artisan caste. Both are accorded ritual status, since their services are related to the goddess of earth as manifested in the land.

Rights and Responsibilities

The Oil-Presser (Ganiga): Shivapur now has no oil-presser of its own. Formerly two Lingayat familes performed the function, but they have now given it up. A Rajaput family also used to do it, but they too have turned to other work. The Ganiga is considered a trader. His ritual status is connected with the notion of pure oil. The villagers used to buy oil from the market even when they had the local oil-presser, but for the oil used in the temple they went only to the village oil-presser, being sure of the purity of his oil.

The Barber (Hadapad): There are 7 households practising the occupation, and all belong to the Lingayat and form one of its sub-castes. Four of the families are immigrants who have come to Shivapur via their kinship ties. The local barber and the immigrant barber are clearly distinguished. One of the immigrants and his son-in-law have set up the only salon in Shivapur which is run on a cash basis. The barbers are *Ayagaras*, each barber family serving from 5 to 25 *Aya-dakulas*. Old men, wealthy men, the priests, caste and Panchayat leaders, and other leading figures invite the barber to do his job at their own homes. The rest usually go elsewhere, and have no fixed place in this respect. The barber's work has a clearly ritual aspect. After a shave or a haircut, one is supposed to be polluted, and a bath is necessary to restore one to normal status. Before a bath one is not allowed to touch pots, pans and especially children. Since the barber's status and his occupation are low, he is associated with pollution. His ritual aspect comes to the fore on ceremonial occasions. The first haircut or the tonsure ceremony is an example. The first haircut from a child is not casually thrown away but is put into a special place. It is considered an offering to god. During the marriage ceremony the bridegroom has to get his hair cut and his face shaved before he can enter the marriage bower. Among the Brahmans, the ceremony of wearing the sacred thread involves a haircut. Among Brahmans as well as Marathas, death calls for a haircut for the nearest relations. Among the Brahmans, a widow must have her head shaved ceremonially. For his services in such ceremonies, the barber is given the *ulipi*.

The Washerman (Agasa): There are 12 households of Washermen, each serving from 5 to 35 *Ayadakulas*. For every Washerman, a fixed quantity of grain is paid for traditional services. Washing the clothes of guests is considered extra work for which extra payment has to be made. Extra services performed on festive or other ceremonial occasions have also to be paid for separately. Normally, dirty clothes are collected on Wednesdays and returned on Mondays. The job of collecting and returning clothes is usually done by women and children. Men wash men's clothes and women women's. A man would consider it below his dignity to wash black cloth, i.e., women's. Children from 6 years onwards begin participating in the work of the families. The barber as well as the washerman are given food, usually the jawar cake (*Rotti*), on the day they perform their services. The washerwoman's specific services include those at the birth of a child. The mother is considered ritually unclean during the first twelve days after delivery. The washing done during this period is not considered extra, but any work done thereafter is regarded as extra. In the second week, the washerwoman is given a blouse-piece and rice given in the fold of the saree (*Udiakki*). The first menstruation of a girl is a period of pollution and requires similar services. For the first 12 days after first menstruation, a girl is not allowed to strain herself by moving about. She is isolated, fed with rich food and showered with gifts. Women gather round her and sing songs. The puberty saree is given away as a gift to the washerwoman. At marriage, during the rite of *Guggala*, a ritual procession is supposed to go from the bride's home to the temple. The priest does not walk on bare ground, but on cloth. The washerman who spreads white cloth, the *Hadadi*, on which the priest moves, is honoured with the gift of a dhoti and turban, and his wife is given a saree. Similar spreading of cloth is required during the ceremony of fulfilling a vow made to a deity. Then, too, the washerman is paid extra. Village festivals or communal feasts such as those for invoking the rain are celebrated by a ceremony in which the owner of Basava (Bull-God) is taken over a path covered with *Hadadi*. Here again the washerman's services are regarded as extra. At the time of death, the washerman washes the clothes of the dead man as well as those of the person attending the funeral ceremony. For this service he is given gifts of plates, pots and pans. As usual, on all festive occasions, he is offered the gift of grain.

The Village Servant/Labourer (Barikar): Before the emergence of the Panchayat, he had the function of lighting the streets, cleaning the temple verandahs, and of acting as a receptionist to the village office. Now, of course, these duties do not form part of his services. There are now 5 Barikar households in Shivapur. The Barikar worships in the Lingayat temples and also that of the high-caste Hindus. He does not serve the mosque. The most important focus of his worship is the temple of Basava (Bull-God). On festive occasions, he is the one to help in giving an oil-bath to the image in the temple. It is his job to decorate the temple door with a string around which are tied mango leaves. This is supposed to signify an auspicious occasion. During the festival of *Basava Jayanti*, he is the one to decorate the street corners with cords from which dangle the mango leaves. During public feasts arranged as part of a vow-fulfilling ceremony, he cleans the utensils of the temple. During the marriages of the high-castes he cleans the utensils, does the decoration of hanging mango leaves from strings, and attends to the cattle of the guests by fetching them fodder, water, etc. At the time of death it is his job to get leaves of a special kind with which the bier is decorated and without which the bier cannot move. During the pregnancy rites, he is always round the corner to perform odd errands. All

5 households of the Barikars are related. The Barikar is, in a sense, close to the life of the *Ayadakula*, since he is allowed to wash such intimate items as cooking pots and pans. At the same time his lower status is more than indicated in the practice that after he has cleaned them the utensils are washed again ritually. He is entitled to his *Aya* and also fodder for his cattle during all important occasions.

The Barikars in the village are the only functionaries who are completely landless. An old Barikar, Makkappa, complained that his was the only landless caste in Shivapur. He narrated the story of how, years ago, a District Officer had promised him land if he could find any. Makkappa did show a piece of common land, but the villagers stood in his way by declaring that the land in question was required for common grazing.

The Instrumental Musicians (Koravas): They are also known as the Bajantries. There are 11 of their households in the village. Three of these households, till recently, formed one family, but have now split up. They perform the traditional service of playing music in the traditional style. Their services are made available to individual families as well as to the village community as a whole. If there is an unusually important birth, either because of the status of the family or because of the importance of the event itself (e.g. if a first male child is born after a long time), the musicians are invited to provide music. But such occasions are rare. More frequently their music is requisitioned for marriages and deaths. On these occasions the families concerned invite them to play the music. For these services they expect to be given a fixed payment. It is not so much that it is precisely fixed as that there is a clear expectation as to what is to be paid. In addition to such payments, they are also paid the *Kusi*, a free gift induced by the prevailing mood of the occasion.

Though in one sense the Koravas are not *Ayagaras*, they are nevertheless drawn into the system. Though they do not go about collecting grain regularly like the *Ayagaras*, they are invariably given grain whenever they ask for it on festive and important occasions. They also make basketry and mats, but this work is mostly performed by the women. This supplements the income of the Koravas. On important festive occasions like the *Nagarapanchami* (festival of snakes), the *Deepavali* (festival of lights) and the *Ugadi* (New Year's Day), the Koravas go round the village, from house to house, playing music. This service is not given to anyone in particular, but is a traditional one to the village as a whole. There is no payment for this service, but they are given food.

The Koravas serve all the village gods and goddesses except those belonging to the untouchables. Though all the Korava families have land, they are not primarily cultivators since the land owned is too small, each holding being generally less than half an acre. The Koravas hire the bullocks from the farmers when necessary, and, in return, they offer their musical services. In the month of May, the Lingayats have a bullock procession, and the Koravas play music for it. For this service they are paid since it is performed at individual request. Their music is offered in the service of all gods and goddesses, excepting those of the untouchables, and prominent among these are Durgavva, Dyamavva, the village Basava and the Basava on the hillock, Ramalinga, and Banashankari. They also serve in the mosque, where they give music free, since they are located near the Muslim area and are dependent on them. Even though they are not strictly *Ayagaras*, they go to the harvest pit and collect grain. Lastly, they provide yet another link in the inter-village relationships. Their services are made available in four talukas of one district as well as in two entire districts. For such services they get a fixed payment, not *Aya*. The music offered by the Koravas is highly traditional and sacred in style, and it differs sharply from the secular music of the bands. The latter have incorporated tunes from the music of the films.

Rights and Responsibilities

The Village Servant (Talawar): There are 25 households belonging to the Talawars in the village. The Talawar is the traditional servant of the village. He carries the messages for the Panchayat. But today, and at least in Shivapur, he is mainly a labourer or agriculturist.

The Untouchable (Holeya or Madar): They have two sub-groups—the Cheluvadi and the Madiga. There are 5 households, consisting of 25 members, of the Cheluvadis, and 12 households, consisting of 41 members, of the Madigas. The Madigas are further distinguishable into the local (Idduru) and immigrant (Paravuru) Madigas. The Cheluvadis are superior to the Madigas and the local Madigas superior to the immigrant Madigas. 3 Madiga households have migrated to Dharwar.

The Cheluvadis are the traditional sweepers. It is their job to bring the carcasses of animals to the Madigas, who keep half back for their leather-work, and return the other half to the Cheluvadis, who sell it in the market. Formerly the Cheluvadis also used to make leather goods, although as a rule they no longer do so. They carry the message of death.

Each Cheluvadi is dependent on the *Ayadakula* families of 5 to 13. During *Ganapati* (Elephant God) festival, *Basava Jayanti* celebrations and the *Karahunnime* celebrations, they supply the red earth with which the cattle shed is traditionally smeared. During the marriage time, the Cheluvadis look after the cattle of the guests, chop the fuel wood and remove the dung. During the harvest time they are around the threshing floor, ready to do all sorts of odd jobs for the farmer. They assist in the digging of the grain storing pit (*Hage*). At the time of birth their services are not called for, as they are considered inauspicious and polluted. At death, they are required to beat the doleful drum which accompanies the funeral procession. As part of this ceremony there is a gift-basket which the Cheluvadis carry. The Cheluvadis are not given measured grain, but *Aya*. The regard with which these untouchables are traditionally treated may be seen from the fact that they are seldom denied when they ask for something. This may be an index of the degree to which the farmers depend upon the services of the Cheluvadis. On all important occasions, not less than six a year, they collect food which is specially set apart for them. They usually collect it in the evening.

At the harvest time each Cheluvadi household gets from 4 to 5 bags of jawar. The tendency to draw the untouchables into the social matrix may be clearly perceived in the practice of the ceremony of wearing 'the green bangles of the family' (*Balagada Bale*). This involves the gift of green bangles at the time of marriage. It is given to the Cheluvadis and Madigas, as also to the washerman and the potter. The priests of the village do not go personally to attend on them. The Cheluvadis and Madigas have their own barber and their own gods. However, they worship the other gods too, whereas none worships their gods. Even the Muslim god is worshipped by the untouchables. When one examines the kind of services performed by the untouchables, one realises that essentially they are cast in the role of carriers of sin and pollution. The presents they receive vary according to the context. Among the Cheluvadis there is a woman who practises temple (religious) prostitution, and her daughter also does so.

As for the Madigas, they form the lowest stratum of the social-economic hierarchy. The untouchables as a whole live outside the main area of the village. While the Cheluvadi settlement is on the left, that of the Madigas lies to the right. Among the Madigas there is only one family of agriculturists, which owns 2 acres of land. Every Madiga household depends on 5 to 12 *Ayadakulas*. Their functions and privileges are virtually similar to those of the Cheluvadis, though they are ranked lower. At the harvest time they get 3 to 5 bags of jawar. The only difference between them and the Cheluvadis is that they are leather-workers while the latter are sweepers. The Madiga keep the *Ayadakulas* supplied with all their leather requirements. Sweeping is ranked higher occupationally than leather-work. Moreover, the Madigas eat the meat of the dead animals while the Cheluvadis do not. This also lowers their status. The Madigas have their own gods. They practise endogamy.

3

Having given a detailed descriptive account of the occupational groups, we may consider some general questions. It may be noted that in the *Aya* system of Shivapur, the right to serve and the right to claim *prestations* are implied in the texture of social life itself and not insisted upon. If either of the participants in a transaction fails to live up to the implied expectations, the incident is immediately known to the entire village. Thus the parties are careful not to transgress the inexplicit, but none the less obligatory, limits of social prescription. In cases of transgression when a person works more and gets less, the aggrieved party throws subtle hints of resentment, indicated by sulking. If the transgression is still persisted in, the *Ayagara* deserts the *Ayadakula*. A landless man may deny the farmer a service if he has a reason. The artisans, for instance, may refuse service to a farmer, and thus bring him down. This is, of course, an extreme situation in which the system breaks down.

The dependence of the economically well-to-do on the economically less well-off is as great as that of the latter upon the former. The system rests on the principle that none is dominant and all are liable to be brought down. In Shivapur, the wealthy are not concentrated in a single caste, but are dispersed. Social behaviour is regulated by accepted principles. Everyone is aware of his position and of what he may or may not do. In consequence, one finds in Shivapur a general eagerness to respect each other's rights and obligations. The transactions involving rights and responsibilities form an endless chain, from the priest down to the Madiga, and the sustaining principle is the essential interdependence of everybody on everybody.

Rights and Responsibilities

All are equal, each in a special way, since all have their legitimate rights and responsibilities. As already noted, if one gives less and takes more, there is avoidance and even desertion. But this kind of transgression does not go on endlessly. It has limits, since at the point at which it tends to undermine the social foundation, social forces assert themselves and restore normality. If one gets inside the mental workings of the people, one notes that none in Shivapur thinks overtly in terms of caste or status. The categories that prevail are normal/abnormal. To behave in accordance with *Dharma* is normal, and to violate *Dharma* is abnormal. If one behaved abnormally one would be legitimately putting oneself beyond the pale of village society, and indeed out of all social existence.

V

STRENGTH AND VALUES

I

THE ECONOMY OF Shivapur as exemplified in the *Aya* system is one based on exchange of gifts. It is neither too rigid nor closed. It is not too rigid because it allows for additional gifts as well as additional work involving additional payment. The driving force behind this system is custom, and the principle governing the various social relations is mutual understanding and co-operation. The type of economy we are examining presupposes a cultural pattern in which the dominating theme is close and inevitable interdependence. This is clearly manifested in the configuration of the various inter-relations of groups and institutions in Shivapur. We have, for instance, the caste-occupation inter-relationship in which caste/sub-caste groups invariably aggregate round occupational nuclei. The priestly occupation has given rise to the priestly caste; the occupation of a carpenter involves a carpenter caste; the occupations of the goldsmith and blacksmith lead to corresponding caste groups; and so on. This inter-relationship is illustrated by the Lingayat family, which has taken to blacksmithing, having formed an endogamous sub-caste of its own.

Then we have close inter-relations between economic and religious factors. The institution of temple lands is an area where there is co-ordination between religious and economic factors. The relations between higher and lower castes are as much economic as religious. The notions of purity and pollution associated with occupations and the notion

74

of sin associated with non-performance of traditional occupational activities, involving the idea of *Dharma*—all these indicate how intimately economics and religion are connected. Finally, we have inter-relations between the economy and kinship. The Shivapur economic system works as it does partly because of the kinship relations that function. We have cases in which families of craftsmen immigrate to the village via kinship relationships, and eventually get accepted as part of the local economic pattern. The nature of certain occupations like farming involves a considerable number of persons, and here kinship ties are a great help.

We have already mentioned that no village is self-sufficient occupationally, and that no village has all the functional groups operating. But such a deficiency of functional groups may have one of two consequences. Either a single occupational group becomes multi-occupational or the village seeks to make good the deficiency by invoking assistance from neighbouring villages. What has actually happened is the latter development, leading to inter-village relations. This is largely because there is an overwhelming customary sanction against people abandoning traditional occupational specialisations. This inter-village pattern, of course, works both ways. Outside specialists are drawn into village life, while local specialists go out to other villages to make good similar deficiencies. In Shivapur every specialist, from the priest down, has his extra-territorial activity, thus radiating a number of inter-village links. This again leads us back to the *leitmotiv* of the *Aya* system of Shivapur, inter-dependence of one villager upon another, and of one village upon another.

When we go on to examine the pattern of the exchange of services in Shivapur, we may isolate types of interdependence. Shivapur is essentially bi-economical, by which we mean that it has an economy based on land and traditional *prestations*, and another economy based on the more modern cash principle. Some of the economic relations between occupational groups relate to the first economy and others to the second economy. The seven types of inter-relations may be briefly listed: 1 Farmer–Farmer, 2 Farmer–Artisan, 3 Farmer–Labourer, 4 Labourer–Labourer, 5 Arti-san–Artisan, 6 Artisan–Labourer, and 7 Priest–Rest of the community. We shall now look at them separately.

1 *Farmer–Farmer*: In Shivapur land is a scarce resource. If one has but an acre of land, one is not in a position to buy all the implements and has to borrow implements, cattle, and bullock-cart from one's more prosperous neighbours. This is a frequent kind of farmer–farmer interdependence. During the harvest time this interdependence is most vividly manifested. One can see at this time a clear operation of the gift system. There are generally five harvest clusters in-stalled in different places, and one can watch the movement of farmers from cluster to cluster in order to assist each other. Each cluster itself is an example of farmer–farmer dependence and co-operation. During this time both im-plements and services are exchanged in mutual interest. When the grain is harvested it has to be carted home. A bullock-cart is not a usual possession, and so farmers invariably borrow the carts from the few who possess them.

2 *Farmer–Artisan*: The whole of the *Aya* system is based on this type of relationship. The farmer depends on the priest, carpenter, blacksmith and so on. In fact, the whole process of agricultural production draws into its heart the services of everyone from the priest down to the untouch-able. The priest has to be consulted for the auspicious time when important agricultural operations may be initiated, the various artisans are required for the production of implements, and the landless and the untouchables are re-quired as labourers. This is a typical and frequent kind of relationship. Its main features have been described in con-nection with our account of the *Aya* system. The relation-

ship here is a dual one. In the first place, there is the *Aya-dakula–Ayagara* pattern in which the former give traditional gifts of grain in exchange for the gift of specialised services offered by the latter.

This pattern is governed by traditional behaviour, and backed up by customary sanctions ultimately involving *Dharma*. Both sides are free to withdraw from their respective roles, if they have grounds for doing so against the other. Secondly, there are additional services outside the traditional exchange of gifts, which have to be paid for in cash. For instance, a carpenter's service in building a house falls outside the traditional, obligatory service, and it has to be paid for separately. Or the washerman irons cloth, and that is also an extra. The blacksmith may make the iron rim for the wheel of a bullock-cart and that is considered an extra.

3 *Farmer–Labourer*: Like land, labour is a scarce commodity in Shivapur. Its strength in bargaining derives from this fact. The farmer depends so much on labour in his occupational activities that he cannot easily tread on its toes and get away with it. During the operation of picking cotton or plucking peanuts, the labourer may refuse to serve if he considers that the farmer has not accorded him adequate respect. He resents ill-treatment by a farmer, and this may and usually does lead to refusal to serve. Moreover, the degree of willingness with which labourers serve a farmer is considered a matter of prestige. In the eyes of the village community, a farmer who can get labour willingly and spontaneously is highly regarded. There are interesting illustrations to show how this may come about. There is a curious practice in Shivapur, according to which the fixing of the ceiling of a house is a service which is normally given free. During weddings, too, the dependent persons belonging to one's own caste are supposed to serve at feasts without demanding payment. But sometimes, because of resentment, such services are refused free, and the prestige of the

farmer who has been denied these traditional free services is considerably lowered in the eyes of the village. This is an indication of the value attached to the goodwill of the labourers. It also points to the highly personal nature of the relationship involved between the farmer and the labourer.

4 *Labourer–Labourer*: Labourers depend on each other in many contexts, and a spirit of spontaneous co-operation prevails among the various types. But this should not be confused with the spirit of modern trade unionism. It is much more personal, far less organised and far more spontaneous. For instance, if a *Jita* labourer is unable to perform his obligatory duties, his brother or someone else in the family volunteers to do them. This is not to be taken simply as an indication of family solidarity, though it is partly that. If one labourer is unable to keep his promise, there is always another labourer who is willing to come to the rescue and offer the necessary service.

5 *Artisan–Artisan*: There is a proverb in Shivapur which says, '*Ayagaras* do not like each other'. Never was a proverb more misleading, for one can observe a remarkable degree of friendly co-operation between different artisans. There are any number of instances in which an artisan is seen to render his services free to another, though it may, in fact, be a kind of exchange of free services. There is a remarkable story of such a relationship between a barber and a carpenter, to which we have already alluded. A local carpenter, eager to establish good-will, gave free help to an immigrant barber in the construction of a house. The barber returned the compliment by offering his services free to the carpenter for life, incidentally conferring on him a special status. When an artisan is ill, fellow-artisans rally round to his support. During the field work for this report, a carpenter fell ill; the other carpenter living next door came to his rescue by doing his work. Among all the types of relationship we have studied, this seems to be the most personal.

Strength and Values

6 *Artisan–Labourer*: The dependence of the labourer on the artisans is quite obvious. The labourer is required to use implements in weeding or in any other agricultural operation. These are made by the carpenter and the blacksmith. Since the artisans also depend on the labourers, they usually do not charge for making small implements, and demand payment only for the larger ones. This sense of interdependence has a moral/ideological aspect in so far as this action is buttressed by the maxim that it is nobler to give a gift freely.

7 *Priest–The Rest*: For the countless ritualistic elements of which the life of Shivapur is essentially made up, the priest is indispensable for all. Thus there is a clear dependence of all upon his sacred functions. This is a normal situation. The priest, on the other hand, depends on the rest for his secular needs. But sometimes the relationship is governed by a more obviously free gesture of giving. There is a priest of the Chikkamath group in Shivapur who has also specialised in medicine. He, in fact, carries on a medical practice as a secondary activity. Recently we came across a case in which this man gave injections to a patient in a farmer's family without charging any fee. The gesture was appreciated, and reciprocated by the farmer in question who freely gave fodder to the priest-cum-medical practitioner. Professionally, the priest is not affected by material-secular values and this is tacitly accepted by the community when it offers him services freely in the material-secular realm. One example may be cited. The Shivapur people observe a custom by which new clothes are not worn before they are washed. The washerman of the village (a Muslim) does this service freely for the priest. When the priest of the Hiremath group happens to pass by a vegetable garden and asks for vegetables, the farmers invariably offer him a free gift. Thus we see the principle of mutual obligation and interdependence at work, but not overtly.

The pattern of relationships indicated above looks symmetrical. But this is so only under ideal conditions; there is a tendency towards asymmetry, due largely to the hierarchical nature of the society as a whole. The landless labourer is an example in this connection. On the whole he is kept at the receiving end only, getting virtually no occasion to give back, so far as the artisans are concerned. Of course, one has to bear in mind the fact that the artisans give, not because they hope to assert their superiority, but because it is part of their duty to give, and also that they expect to receive something in return. Yet, paradoxically, the artisan emerges as a superior person since it is one of the moral axioms of Shivapur that he who gives is superior to him who receives. The superiority of the giver to the receiver, it needs to be emphasised, is accepted irrespective of the caste, economic or social status of the giver. We wish to emphasise this aspect strongly, since we feel that the currently prevalent theory of a dominant caste breaks down, since the relations that we have here mapped are neither predominantly power relations or economic ones.

One of the sources of strength for the *Aya* system is the mode of payment of the gifts. The mode of payment includes both the calendar of payment and the content of payment. First, the calendar of payment may be briefly described. The payments are made annually, half-yearly, monthly/fortnightly and weekly/daily.

The Annual payment: The *Alategalu* (fixed measure of grain) is given annually. The year is reckoned from harvest to harvest, but not precisely. There is not only no actual date fixed, but there is no place fixed where it is to be paid. It may be paid in the harvest field or outside the field. It may even be sent to the home of a receiving party. This payment is received by all, from the priest down to the untouchable. Some of these have the payment sent to wherever they are, but most of the lower castes must collect it at the harvest place. The priest, the carpenter, the blacksmith, the washerman and the barber do not usually go to the field to collect *Alategalu*, but they are sent for to collect it. There are also festivals at which an annual payment is made.

The Half-yearly payment: This is paid during the kharif and rabi harvests. It is given in the form of pulses, vegetables, grain and fruits. It is given when asked. When the harvest pit is dug or when it is cleaned up, these gifts are given to various parties from the carpenter down. The farmer who receives small services in the harvest season is expected to offer gifts in kind.

The Monthly/Fortnightly payment: The reckoning done through the lunar calendar, from the full-moon day (*Hunnime*) to the moonless day (*Amavasye*). Both these points of measurement are religiously and ritualistically important, in Hindu practice. These are both days when either propitiation or appreciation of the great powers beyond is usually done, and this involes a ritual ceremony. The priest, the washerman and the barber are busy at these times, since their services are required for the rituals. The Kuruba who beats the drum and the untouchable who has to look after the cattle are also kept busy on these occasions. *Dakshine* and *Kushi* are regularly given. Especially during the months of August and October, the services of the priests and servants are constantly requisitioned and paid with plenty of gifts.

The Weekly/Daily payment: The priest, the washerman and the barber attend families on certain fixed days in a week and offer their services. The priest performs the worshipping ceremony, eats his food and collects his *Dakshine* on the day he visits the familes. The washerman and the barber perform their duties on the days set apart for them, and collect food. Practically throughout the year they get free food for one service or the other.

Besides these regular, routine occasions, there are special occasions like family rites, festivals, weddings, births and deaths. On these occasions also, gifts are given on a generous scale. So essential is it considered to give gifts on the occasions of birth, marriage and death, that it is not unusual to find families getting heavily into debt for such purposes. Generosity in giving gifts is a matter of prestige on these occasions. The priest is offered food as well as gifts. The washerman, too, gets both food and gifts. The Barikar gets food only. All these, as well as the Hugar and the Mathapati, render distinct services on such occasions. The Hugar supplies the flowers and the Mathapati helps in carrying messages. They all get gifts. In the marriage ceremony the priest is associated at every stage and appropriate gifts are given to him at all stages. The goldsmith, of course, is required to make the wedding ornaments, both ritualistic as well as ostentatious. The carpenter assists in the construction of the ceremonial marriage bower. The Kuruba comes in to beat his lusty drum and the Korava comes in to play his pipes. The potter is required to make the pots which form part of the marriage ceremony. The Mathapati and the Ganachari have their roles to play. The untouchables, too, are drawn in with their manual labour. Thus marriage shows the co-operative teamwork of the village. Death, too, is an occasion of great importance. One's love of the dead person manifests itself in the scale on which one spends on such an occasion. Generosity in giving in such a context is considered very important. The new piece of cloth which shrouds the dead body is later divided as a gift between the priest, the carpenter, the washerman and the untouchable, all of whom have their contributions to make on the occasion. The giving of gifts on the above occasions is common to all castes, Lingayats, Brahmans, Marathas and Muslims.

Now we may turn to the second component of the gift-giving transaction—the content of the gifts. The *Alategalu* is given to all except the priest and the goldsmith. The *Aya* is given to all except the priest. The *Ulipi* is given to the priest, the goldsmith, the carpenter and the washerman, and in fact to all excepting the untouchables, in ritualistic contexts. The *Bab* is offered to the temples on weddings, and during family rites, to all ritual dignitaries of all castes. The carpenter also gets the *Bab* in his capacity as a worshipper of the goddess Dyamavva. The *Nidhi* is given in the same manner as the *Bab*. Other gifts like the *Bandegalu* (grain from the cart), the *Tunda-galu* (the divided grain), the *Habbadakalu* (the grain of the festival), and indeed, grain in all manner of divisions, are given to all. Lastly, the *kushi* is given to all lower servants below and including the washerman. One person may be the recipient of a wide variety of gifts on different occasions. It is strictly not propriety to make overt demands for gifts. If anyone asks, he may get rude replies. He may be asked bluntly whether he knows what the price of grain is.

Though cash transactions of a modern kind are not ruled out, in Shivapur social relations and economic co-operation are not dominated by the money economy. Cases may be cited in which a sense of money is largely absent. There is a goldsmith who lives in a rent-free house belonging to a farmer. There are two washerman families in one of which the farmer has sought to take under his care his widowed daughter and her children, and another where a father-in-law has taken back his daughter-in-law, whom his son-in-law had been unable to maintain, and her children, given them his *Ayadakulas* and helped them run laundries in Dharwar. There are four village teachers from outside who stay with local farmers, whose hospitality they repay by giving tuition to the farmers' children. There is a farmer who has given a piece of land for free use by a barber. These are a few illustrations, and they could be multiplied, of situations in which the mercenary motive is played down. Nonetheless those who receive gifts are governed by the unwritten and instinctively accepted code that you must give more than you receive. Thus every service and every

G   83

courtesy is returned, but in such subtle ways as to escape the notice of all but the most vigilant observer.

3

The dual economy of Shivapur will now be analysed as a dynamic system. An outsider, whether an Indian or a foreigner, looks at the Shivapur economy as a poor, subsistence one, in which land is scarce and opportunities are few because of its closed nature, and generally comes to regard it as characterised by a bitter struggle for existence. However, this is not how the people of Shivapur themselves would look upon their economy. They feel themselves more contented. It is not that they do not want more, but it is simply that they are not unduly worried by their wants. This is not to say that they are passive—far from it. They have crossed even the boundaries of customary sanction in order to supplement their incomes, as may be seen from the fact that secondary occupations, in addition to customary ones, are resorted to. They have also gone beyond the physical boundaries of the village and served neighbouring villages in order to supplement their incomes. This phenomenon has been at the heart of the dual economic system. We can show how this happens with regard to every occupational group.

The Farmer: As already indicated, it is possible to regard the farmer's occupation as dual since he is not only an agricultural producer but also acts as his own market specialist and dealer. A few upper-class farmers have sent at least one son for further education and employment outside the village. There are 17 youths from Shivapur who are employed in various institutions in Dharwar. The children of middle-class farmers go to school in Dharwar, but the interesting point is that each farmer sends just one child for such education. Since the farmers are not altogether unaware of the unemployment problem outside, they are prepared for and make provisions for the absorption of their educated children as well, if necessary.

There is some preceptible urge to turn to education. In this connection an example, not however from a farmer family, may be given. There is in Shivapur a goldsmith who is lazy and does not work. His eldest son, a boy of 12, has taken charge of the traditional work. This youngster supports the whole family. When we asked him what he would wish to be, he replied that he had always wanted to be a supervisor of teachers! He added that since that was not to be, he would educate one of his brothers to take it up, and retain another for the traditional occupation. There is thus a clear tendency on the part of families to look for additional sources, beyond the customary ones, for income.

The Priest: The priests not only perform their duties within the closed village society, but go beyond it to offer their services, for which they get paid. We thus have inter-village priestly services. In this connection, the case of the local Muslim priest (*Mulla*) is very interesting. This man is considered holy and religiously powerful. Miraculous powers have been attributed to him, not only by local people but also from those outside the village. In fact, his reputation has travelled as far as Bombay and Bangalore. A Parsee contractor from Bombay who had sought the mediation of the Mulla in order to gain some benefit in his profession and had actually succeeded, expressed his gratitude by putting up the roof of the mosque at his own expense —incidentally the most imposing structure in Shivapur.

Once the Mulla showed us his watch and said that he got it as a gift. It appears that an agricultural officer from Dharwar had a daughter who was having frequent fits. The Officer, despairing of all other efforts, came to the Mulla, who successfully cured the girl. In appreciation of his services, the officer gave the Mulla the watch. We ourselves had occasion to see how the Mulla composed housewives who had trouble with their mother-in-law and husbands, men and women affected by evil spirits, diseases, etc. He is approached by people of many castes and religions. The Mulla's services in this capacity have been a source of income for himself personally as well as for his mosque.

The Carpenter: Over and above his traditional and customary income via the gift exchanges of the *Aya* system, the carpenter has additional sources of income. A local carpenter who heads a joint family built the big school building and the Panchayat office of Shivapur. This brought him considerable additional income. The chairman of the Panchayat induced him to come forward with a fund of one hundred Rupees, and then the rest had to give as a matter of prestige. The carpenter gets his extra income by building temples and houses in neighbouring villages. When he cannot go himself, he sends his younger brothers.

The Blacksmith: He is a highly skilled artisan who is even reputed to be capable of making country revolvers. Two of his children are studying at school in Dharwar. The eldest son is in the traditional occupation. The second son holds a Diploma in Foundry work and has been employed at the Hindustan Machine Tools Factory at Bangalore, an undertaking of the Central Government. One of the younger sons is being groomed for the traditional occupation. The family owns hardly 3 acres of land, and it is not possible to maintain a family of 6 and to educate children on this primary income. When I asked him how he could manage it, he replied that there were enough additional sources of income. The bifurcation of the occupational pattern within a family illustrates the principle of dualism. It also illustrates how the old and the new ways are co-ordinated, and how the themes of tradition and change are worked into an integrated pattern of social action. Some members of the family are kept back to continue the older occupational pattern while others are sent out to be involved in the more modern type of economic pattern.

The Goldsmith: The fact that there are three immigrant families of goldsmiths in Shivapur is sufficient indication of the spatial mobility of the artisans. This means that they can be on the move, making extra earnings. Two sons of a local goldsmith are primary school teachers, working away from Shivapur, and another is retained to carry on the traditional occupation. An interesting fact to note is that the two primary school teachers do the traditional work when they are in Shivapur for vacations. This is also, incidentally, an indication of the links between tradition and change. The goldsmith is also a painter and a sculptor, and his work in these fields fetches him additional income. He was the one who painted the image of the goddess Dyamavva which, by the way, was completed at about the same time as this field-work. He is the artisan who carved the stone image of the local Maratha temple. He has also performed similar services in villages round about.

The Florist (Hugar): Apart from supplying flowers on ceremonial occasions, he has specialised in making the wedding crown of flowers (*Bashinga*) worn by the bridegroom. This brings him his additional income. He gets a fixed payment for making a *Bashinga*. In one year, he told us, he had made 12 *Bashingas* for five villages. He is a childless man, and according to Hindu belief he should be considered inauspicious and thus not associated with a marriage function. But actually, he is highly praised and in great demand. People refer with approval to his *Kaiguna* (the skill inherent in his hand—a divine gift).

Instrumental Musican (Korava): The Koravas are the traditional musicians who use the pipes. They earn extra money when they perform at the invitation of individual parties. The payment for their services for recreational purposes is fixed, though their services offered on religious occasions are not fixed. They are in demand in the neighbouring villages, and thus they are able to earn extra income. In a single year, these households belonging to one lineage, jointly working, were able to perform their music at 10 marriages during the season (i.e. April/May) in the surrounding villages. Each family earned about one hundred and fifty Rupees in all. Besides such extra earning, the women of the family, who specialise in basketry, earn something on their own to supplement the family income.

The Washerman: The traditional obligation of the washerman is over if he does what is called *Nirmadi,* mere washing of the clothes in water; ironing is regarded as an extra service for which the washerman gets additional income. The ironing of clothes is a luxury which only upper-class farmers can afford. Two of the local washermen have set up laundries in Dharwar, earning round about one hundred Rupees per month each. In this connection it may be noted that the washermen of Dharwar give dirty clothes for washing to Shivapur washermen, who are hired for the purpose. This additional work brings in extra income to the local washermen.

The Barber: The barber gets paid both on the traditional and on a cash basis. In addition to his traditional services, he also renders services to those who pay him cash. The owner of the salon is busy the whole morning, and his job brings him good remuneration compared to other barbers in the village.

The Untouchable (*Holeya*): One Cheluvadi is employed in a nearby urban centre on the railways, and one is a porter at the railway station. Two of them work as sweepers in Dharwar. Three households of Madigas, specialising in leather-work, have migrated to nearby Dharwar. They get locally all kinds of jobs which are a source of additional income. They are employed in road-making and house construction. The *Aya* that an untouchable gets is roughly enough to sustain him half the year. Hence, he seeks and gets extra work to make good the gap between traditional income and necessary expenditure. An important thing to note here is that generally as one moves down the social scale, one finds an ever greater number of family members forced to earn on their own. Among the lower groups and classes, women and children are involved in agricultural work like harvesting, picking and sowing. The untouchables and other lower groups like the Kurubas get extra work both inside and outside the village, and thus manage to make extra income. This service is outside the traditional pattern of occupations.

There is another aspect of the work pattern which requires a brief notice. This is the relationship between work, on the one hand, and factors like age and sex, on the other. One of the most human and humane things about Shivapur life is that all, irrespective of sex, age or physical limitations, are considered, and made to feel, necessary. In all families of all caste/sub-caste groups, every member of the family is drawn into the economy of the family. The elder children look after the younger when the parents are away in the fields or otherwise occupied. The children also assist in feeding the cattle. They help their mother in milking the cow. The sister looks after the baby brother's feeding and toilet habits. This is clearly a major reason why the legislation of the State Government providing for compulsory primary education may not succeed in practice, whatever its ideological justification.

The services of children for the benefit of their own families are non-paid and personal, but for that reason their role in the family economy ought not to be neglected. The older members of a family also look after the younger children. They lull them to sleep and keep watch over them. Moreover, their august presence with its suggestion of experience and the tested wisdom of years is psychologically a very comforting phenomenon in a family. The old are made—and this is more important than mere physical support—to feel till the last moment of their lives that they are wanted.

Equally humane is the treatment given to the physically handicapped. They are also made to feel wanted. Their services are utilised during the harvest time when situations needing more sedate activities are not wanting.

The women are considered important as workers. The general rule is that one marries a wife below one's social status, in which case she could be asked to work. Among all castes, the coming of a new bride is welcomed on severely utilitarian grounds. She is bound to be helpful in cooking, in bringing water, and even in assisting in the traditional occupation of the household. In picking cotton, collecting dirty clothes for washing, in looking after cattle, in making basketry, in dusting, in cleaning pots and pans, women are needed. Among the untouchables, women specialise as sweepers while men work as labourers. Thus the crucial role played by women in the economy of the family is obvious.

4

Suppose one were to ask, wherein lies the strength and durability of the social system? An answer to such a question would have to be complex and would have to take into account a number of factors.

The system promises security for all. Land is not the only source of income, and there are other sources which buttress the economy. A sense of security is further strengthened by the fact that everyone is made to feel, and himself feels, that he is essential. This keen mutual dependence creates an emotional climate of security for all. If one looks at the pattern of social behaviour from different angles, one sees how everyone's actions and services are knit with everybody else's actions and services into an enduring social fabric.

The sense of social obligation on the part of the economically better-off comes to the fore when an occasion calls for it. In this connection a very telling story may be narrated. We have already said that there is considerable population pressure on land here. For the last two years rains had been scarce, and the village tanks and wells had just about dried up. All this had led to an acute food scarcity in the village. Indeed, this had been a national problem which had been tackled by setting up government trading in food grains and by American aid. But Shivapur had tried to solve it in its own way and within its traditional ideological framework. Incidentally, the story may underscore the survival strength of our village society. As mentioned above, when we went there for field-work, the days were grim, haunted by the spectre of famine. One day we saw a person belonging to the lower-class hurrying with a pouch made of his dhoti. He looked cheerful. Later on, it turned out that an ordinary middle-class farmer was distributing free food grains to local labourers, irrespective of whether they were his *Ayagaras* or not. The grain so distributed was worth Rs. 1000, an astonishingly huge amount in relation to the village economy. The following morning Shivapur hit the headlines of the local press, when the generosity of the farmer became news.

The sense of security does not arise simply from the size or quantity of land a man may possess. The very fact that one owns land, however small in size, produces a feeling of security. Land is thus a source of security, and the strength of the social order is to some extent based on it.

The institutions of family and kinship have also contributed their share to the strength and stability of the social system. The extended family has proved to be an ideal institution for the kind of social and economic system which the village has evolved. Everyone, the landed and the landless, reaps the benefit of the joint family. Normally, the joint family is supposed to be ideal only for landed families, but in our experience it has been a source of strength to landless families as well, such as those of the artisans. As has been said elsewhere, the bulk of village opinion favours the continuance of the joint family. Yet the institution has suf-

fered considerably in recent years. This is due not so much
to any individualistic ideology as to the cumulative consequences of a number of causes such as deaths in a family,
family quarrels, economic factors, accommodation diffi-
culties, and so on.

Then there is a widespread feeling of kin-mindedness.
One always goes to the rescue of one's kinsmen in diffi-
culties. Widows, old persons and the physically handicapped are not discarded, but given protection. This feeling
for kinship is not confined to the local society, since it cuts
across the village boundaries. The kinship principle underlies the practice in which the *Ayagara* as well as the *Ayadakula* are inherited. The goldsmith, the carpenter and the
washerman have inherited their *Ayadakula*. Since patri-
locality is predominant, this has brought in immigrants to
the village through marital alliances. This has also strengthened the local economic system.

Lastly, we have the links forged between political and
economic factors. All the population in Shivapur is classifi-
able into lineages. The lineage dominates the street society
since normally one lineage dominates one street. Yet the
lineage loyalty is subordinated to the village interest. Moreover, in some streets the residents are mixed up, and this
has not strengthened lineage loyalty. The street is politically
important, since votes at the Panchayat elections are cast
largely along caste lines. The voting pattern has an economic aspect as well. We have already cited the case of a
carpenter who, because of a feeling of resentment at ill-
treatment refused to vote for his *Ayadakula*. Thus we may
see in political behaviour a fusion of caste, economics and
politics.

5

We may now briefly summarise the values that sustain the
social order in Shivapur. First, we have economic security.
The system, as we have shown, is designed to create as much
economic security as is possible within the framework of

other values. Economic security is further guaranteed by the secondary and supplementary sources of work. Secondly, work is highly valued. No individual or group can maintain itself without making an adequate contribution to social existence in all its various aspects. Thirdly, tradition is regarded as the highest value and sanction. Everything is handed down by tradition. One's occupation, one's obligations and even one's customers are all handed down from generation to generation. The *Ayagaras* inherit their *Ayadakula* as much as the latter inherit the former. This right of inheriting *Ayagaras* or *Ayadakula* applies equally to men and women.

Fourthly, one of the intangible and unmeasurable values governing the social relations is highly personal. A particular pattern is sustained because it links the participants in a purely personal relationship. Social institutions of service here are quite unlike the modern, impersonal ones such as the bank, the co-operative society, etc. Some such institutions introduced here have failed since they do not adjust to the local ethos. It is significant that the oldest co-operative unit here, which is half a century old, has failed to enthuse or involve the people of Shivapur to a serious extent.

Fifthly, the basic value that underlies all social relations is co-operation, not competition. This may be seen in almost every context of life, especially when a near conflict arises. The system tends to encourage compromises. Its prevailing spirit is quite unlike that of the modern, free, economic society of the competitive market.

Sixthly, there is a driving force of integration which tends to fuse every aspect with every other aspect. One notes a fusion of social, political, economic and religious forces at all levels. The *Aya* system itself is a total whole which has integrated these manifold aspects of life.

Seventhly, the ultimate sanction of everything is custom, whether formally institutionalised or operating informally. It may operate through the institution of councils or merely through informal gossip, censure and praise.

Lastly, one may derive all sanctions from the cosmic order of *Dharma*. *Dharma* is the highest value which sustains all. To violate it is, accordingly, the highest offence. But *Dharma* itself is supposed to work through social custom. As a belief-generating value, however, *Dharma* has the highest status. *Dharma* is, of course, linked with other complementary notions like *Karma*, *Papa* (sin), *Punya* (merit). The distinctive role of *Dharma* is to anchor the temporal in the eternal, and thus elevate life to an essential, permanent ritual.

VI

CONFLICTS AND TENSIONS

I

IF SOCIAL LIFE is made possible by the existence of similar
and dissimilar interests, this is a situation which is potentially
capable of leading to conflicts and tensions. All societies,
since that is inherent in the very fact of being together, tend
at some time or other towards conflicts and tensions. In a
simple society such conflicts do not often arise, whereas in a
more sophisticated and complex society there are more frequent occasions for conflict and the consequent tensions.
But no society, however rudimentary, is entirely free from
such eventualities. Since these are conflicts inherent in
social systems, their nature cannot be grasped unless one
sees them in the right perspective. This requires that at the
least one must relate these conflicts and tensions to the
general social structure which generates them, and to the
values which lie at the foundation of that structure.

Such a perspective implies the need for what may be
called the 'inside' experience. If one merely views these
conflicts and tensions as an outsider and without properly
placing them in their context, one is liable to misunder-
stand their very nature. In the case of the *Aya* system,
Western observers have fallen into the latter trap, and much
Indian sociological thinking has been influenced by the
Western viewpoint. This is indeed a regrettable state of
affairs. However, we should add that the 'inside' point of
view is also susceptible to another kind of trap—that of
reaching a degree of absorption in the material studied

which would prove detrimental to a scientific understanding of it. To keep oneself clear of these two dangers is a hard task, but it has to be done if one is to reach a true insight into the working of societies as integrated wholes, not merely as assemblages of separately perceived data.

To understand such conflicts and tensions as develop within Shivapur social life can scarcely be done unless one has a clear understanding of certain key concepts which operate as the leading themes of social life. These are the concepts of exchange, property and service. They are highly loaded terms culturally. If the conflicts and tensions of Shivapur are seen in terms of such basic, cultural concepts, one can make sense of them. The *Aya* system, like all social systems, has its share of conflicts and tensions. They may be classified broadly as those arising at the individual, group and community levels. Obviously there is bound to be some overlapping. We now offer a few details bearing on these levels, and indicate their causes.

In Shivapur one's caste determines one's occupation, one's social/economic status, and the rituals one is called upon to perform in the course of one's life. When the individual transgresses the rules of marriage, kinship, occupation and ritual, his life is plunged into conflict with the social mores, thus leading to acute tensions. The case of a local Brahman is to the point. A Brahman is by birth and caste a priest, a priest of the higher caste. Of the three Brahman brothers of Shivapur one has taken to tailoring and another to agriculture. The one who retains some of the priestly functions caters to the religious needs of the lower castes. All these are clearly cases of violation of the Shivapur social order. This has dislocated the Brahman's position in that order, and has led to considerable tension in the lives of the individuals in question. Two individuals with the same occupation may head towards a conflict. For instance, a priest may antagonise another priest by serving the families which are traditionally in the other's charge. Here the interests of the individuals which have come into conflict are a complex mixture of social, economic and ritualistic elements.

Land, as has often been repeated in these pages, is a scarce commodity. This in itself is a sufficiently rich source of conflict between individuals. The smaller farmers are naturally dependent on the bigger farmers for a number of things. But this dependence of the lower on the higher is a phenomenon that exists at all levels throughout the hierarchical line of Shivapur social structure. This dependence may, and often does, lead to a sense of resentment or discontent on the part of the dependent against the person on whom he depends. This is a clear situation of conflict and tension. The acute helplessness of the dependent is further heightened by the fact that there are very few and limited escape routes in this largely closed economic system. The tensions do not easily come out into the open, but simmer within.

Another source of conflict is the impact of competition from outside. As we have suggested, the value highly cherished by this society is co-operation, not competition. But since it is only a highly closed, not a completely closed, system, there is scope for external forces of competition. In the place of the traditional situation of co-operative dependence, the modern situation of the competitive market is brought about. The bigger families are in a position to sell their produce in the competitive market outside and thus make money. The smaller farmer may be unable to follow suit. This leads to conflict and tension. The local goldsmith, the oil-grinder and the washerman are drawn into a competitive relationship with their opposite numbers in the nearly urban centres like Hubli or Dharwar. The local people have access to the services of outside artisans as well as the Shivapur ones. This leads to competition between the two sets of artisans. The competition is rather unequal, since the urban artisan is in a more advantageous position. He can sell his more standardised goods at a lower price, and this naturally leads to tension. The shoeshop or the laundry in the towns can offer better service at a lower price.

Another source of tension between individual and individual arises when there is a failure of crops due to shortage of rainfall. If the pre-harvest rains do not come, this destroys the crops. When such misfortunes arrive, the harvest time turns out to be a time of tensions. The sense of tension is accentuated by the presence of prayer meetings known as *Bhajanamandals* (the Bhajan groups organised to offer devotionals songs), which sing themselves hoarse in order to invoke the gods to give them their gift of rain. The times of scarcity are very bad times indeed! The farmers in Shivapur are not normally given to hoarding grain. They may stock it on a small scale for purposes of future consumption, but that is quite a different matter. There is here no motive of making money out of a general misfortune. But the atmosphere is such that farmers are goaded into keeping grain in order to fend against worse times expected to follow. This adds to the tenseness of the atmosphere and men become easily persuaded to quarrel on even trivial grounds. But these are short-term sources of conflict and tensions.

Then we have more basic sources of such tensions, created by larger causes. Among these and very important is population pressure. In Shivapur, while the birth-rate has not risen, the death-rate has declined, thanks to modern sanitary and medical facilities. On the one hand, this has created population pressure. On the other hand, it has raised other kinds of population problems. In relation to the number of farmers, the number of artisans has increased appreciably. The position of the land has further added to the problem. The prevailing tenancy laws, designed to give the tenant a fair deal and to eliminate absentee landlordism, imply that the owner, unless he cultivates himself, must sell his land, and further, he must sell it only to those who cultivate the land in question.

Property which once belonged to a single owner has now come to be split up between small owners who are ex-tenants. This has speeded up the process of fragmentation of land. Prior to these laws, the fragmentation of land generally occurred at the break-up of joint families. The final upshot of all this has been to increase the number of small farmers with very limited resources, which has obviously made for tension.

Then there are ideological factors which are both economic and political. The initiation of the Community Development movement has introduced new values and ideals to Shivapur. As part of this movement, the village has acquired a common tank, a common school, and so on. But the use of these new amenities is governed by the new egalitarian ideology. All groups, irrespective of the traditional hierarchical status, are, in theory, equally eligible for these benefits. At school, the untouchable children are officially not segregated, though there are subtle patterns of traditional distinction still in existence. The youth clubs, also part of the new socio-economic programmes sponsored by the government require that all young persons get together. These egalitarian forces and ideas have necessarily come into conflict with the traditional system of 'inequality', sustained by regulated social distance. The old way of doing things is being considerably disturbed, and this is a situation that has possibilities of conflict.

Another facet of the new government policies, the *Panchayat* system, has led to a similar result. This has also brought the egalitarian ideals into the political arena. The traditional habit of assigning lower status to the lower castes and to womenfolk, in particular, has come into sharp conflict with the new set-up. The *Panchayati* system insists on representation for these groups, and thus members of lower castes as well as women mingle equally with the rest in its activities. An allied factor is the policy of the government, both central and state, to provide for reservation of places for untouchables in employment. About 3 Cheluvadis and 5 Madigas of Dharwar have taken advantage of it and migrated from Shivapur to take up employment elsewhere.

Conflicts and Tensions

One sees that with increasing frequency the new egalitarian ideas are coming into conflict with traditional caste values.

Caste, which is the very basis on which the whole *Aya* system rests, is questioned by the new ideology of equality, which is pumped into the village by agencies like the press and the radio. But despite the new values brought from outside, caste continues to grow stronger. Though the traditional caste councils cannot enforce their decisions and are deprived legally of their competence to excommunicate, their hold on the lives of the people remains effective. However, the tussle between the caste councils and the *Panchayati* system has given rise to tensions in the area of economic activities.

The *Aya* system is by its very nature such that it gives rise to conflicts. As we have seen, one of its basic features is that mutual obligations between transacting parties are not explicitly or precisely stated. As already mentioned, the *Aya* itself means 'unmeasured payment'. For such a system to work, the general level of fair-mindedness must be very high. In Shivapur it is high, but lapses cannot be ruled out. There is scope for exploitation, and this would lead to conflicts and tensions. The parties are not aware of the exact quantities to be received or given. Thus the system operates in an atmosphere of imprecision and uncertainty. Besides, everything is done on a personal level and every service is, in a sense, a monopoly. This again adds to the sense of uncertainty. If the barber who is one's *Ayagara* loses his razor, one's haircutting and shaving has to be held up until he manages to get a new razor!

Not only does the system function in a penumbra of uncertainty, it also lacks flexibility. Though *Aya* is not supposed to be fixed, it is broadly fixed by custom in the sense that expectations are more or less clear. But custom had fixed them, at what time none knows exactly: whenever it was, it must have been different from current times. In consequence, what was perhaps reasonable for one set of circumstances may prove to be inadequate under a different set of circumstances. While the cost of living has been shooting up, the *Aya* has remained fixed. The point was effectively made by a carpenter who bitterly complained that while the *Ayadakulas* are earning more, the *Aya* that they give is fixed. The *Ayadakulas* have made things worse by showing open resentment at any overt demand for more *Aya*. I have heard that when an *Ayagara* asks for more, the *Ayadakula* rudely reply, 'Do you know that the cost of grain has gone up sharply?' Thus there is no mechanism for revising the payments. This leads, naturally, to a situation in which conflicts and tensions arise.

The traditional system insists on a rigid and fixed occupational structure. Each man is virtually born to an occupation. This sense of rigidity is further enhanced by the lack of spatial mobility. Since the people, in view of links forged by modern transport, are enabled to see how things are outside, this leads to a sense of despair and helplessness. In Shivapur, there is plenty of labour in the off-seasons, and this leads to tension among labourers. In the full agricultural seasons, labour becomes scarce, and this creates another kind of tension. Now it is the employers who may come into conflict over a scarce commodity. Moreover, the proportion of *Ayadakulas* to *Ayagaras* is not uniform. One *Ayagara* may have as many as 35 *Ayadakulas*, while another may have as few as 5. There is thus inequality in the range of customers available to different *Ayagaras*. This too may lead to conflicts and tensions. Then there is the presence of a group which is almost wholly landless: the Barikars, who are rather unhappy about it.

Moreover, there are factors which are not exclusively locatable in the village itself, for example, the constantly rising spiral of prices and the consequent rise in the cost of living. The accessibility of the modern-style open market to the village also brings its own share of conflicts. The cash economy has disturbed the local economy. Indeed it seems to be on the increase. The well-to-do farmers now prefer to raise cash crops like cotton, groundnuts, fruits and potatoes, which link them with far-away markets. There is a good flow of money from outside. Thus a conflict is set up between the traditional economy of gift exchanges and the modern cash economy. For instance, the artisan groups get considerable scope to operate and take advantage of the cash economy. They are enabled to be increasingly independent of the traditional *Aya* system. This is one of the potential social areas of conflict and tension.

Lastly, one comes across considerable inter-caste tension boiling beneath the surface. A clue to this is the prevalence of proverbs flung at each other by various caste groups and which are picturesquely critical and pungent. A few representative samples are offered here on the assumption that language habits provide clues to the values and modes of the community using the language. Against the carpenter, the proverb says, 'A carpenter without business would go about sawing a son's bottom'. Against the goldsmith: 'A goldsmith would steal, if he got the chance, his own sister's gold.' Against the Banajiga (a Lingayat sub-caste): 'A Banajiga is the one who would carry a dead donkey.' There is a proverb which strikes two birds with a single arrow—the farmer and the Brahman. It says, 'A Brahman squanders his money on eating while the farmer loses a fortune over litigation'. Against a Sadar (another Lingayat sub-caste): 'A Sadar is no better than an untouchable.' Finally, there is a proverb which reveals the low esteem in which an untouchable is held and thus reflects his low socio-economic status. It says, 'Never trust a Holeya. Sooner or later he will make you yell "Ayyayyo" '. The implications is that he will bring misfortune and grief.

2

In this section a number of case studies will be given to show how conflicts and tensions have actually arisen in Shivapur, and how they have been handled. We shall begin with the priests, and among them the Lingayats first. In

Shivapur, as in most Indian villages, there is the religious festival of publicly drawing the chariot associated with a local deity. The chariot is an imposing, temple-tower-like wooden structure. Somewhere at its centre there is provision for installing the image of the deity. In front of the deity there is a small place for the priest. Recently, a dispute arose as to who should have the privilege of occupying the seat, involving the two top priestly groups, the Hiremaths and the Chikkamaths. The Hiremath's claim was that they belonged to an older, senior lineage, and thus were entitled to grace the seat. Passions ran high, so high indeed that one year the conflict prevented the celebration of the very function of chariot drawing. Two years ago an open conflict was settled, or settled itself, in the sense that the disputed seat was allowed to be left unoccupied!

A dispute was waged over the issue of who should sit on the ceremonial platform seat before the deity in the temple of the Hill Basava. This again involved the Hiremaths and Chikkamaths. In this case a more positive and characteristic-ally easy solution was found. It was proposed to put up two platform seats before the image, at equal distance from the image and of equal height, one each for the priests belong-ing to the contending groups. Among the Brahmans, of whom there are three brothers, a dispute arose as to who should normally perform the priestly functions. Of these brothers, the eldest was primarily a priest, with agricultural work as a secondary occupation. The second brother was primarily an agriculturist. The third took up tailoring sup-plemented by agricultural work. They have become separated and they go round crying each other down. Here again, there is strictly no settlement except that there is a kind of shifting situation depending on the parties' willing-ness to press claims. Yet the situation has been brought under some control by the parties themselves.

Among Muslim priests a dispute arose recently, concern-ing the metal symbols representing the Prophet and other religious figures kept in the house of the chief Mulla. On important religious occasions they are taken out in procession. There is a man specialising in the duty of carrying them, and his name derives from this function. He is called the 'Devaru horava' (the one who carries the gods). When the 'gods' are carried in a colourful procession the people throw offerings like coconuts, bananas, etc., on them. The carrier of 'gods' is the one who picks up whatever touches the 'gods'. But the presents made in the form of cash and ornaments do not go to him, but must be handed over to the mosque. He refused to do this in the face of persistent public demand that he do it. He was ousted from the job. Soon after, the people were divided between those who supported his claims and the others who justified the action against him. The situation became tense, involving the village community as a whole. It was settled by a compromise arrived at through the good offices of an inter-caste council.

In 1956, an enterprising and plucky blacksmith, joined by the carpenters, all belonging to a single lineage, made a momentous decision. They decided to take a deputation to their *Ayadakulas* and ask for (a) a system of fixed quantity of grain payment, and (b) to have this quantity increased considerably in view of the rising cost of living. The deputation made the demand, but the farmers first refused it. Later on, the farmers met and made a collective decision of their own to the same effect. The parties persisted in their respective positions, thus creating a tense state of affairs in the village. But gradually it was allowed to go underground. No formal settlement was arrived at just then. But the artisans were biding their time. When the harvest season came, they refused to serve the farmers. This took the farmers completely by surprise. But there was nothing they could do about it. They badly needed the services of the artisans anyway. At first the farmers attempted to coax artisans from outside the village to offer their services. The outside artisans who saw what was going on in the village were unwilling to 'rat' on fellow-artisans. They refused to work. With great difficulty the farmers succeeded in getting hold of one carpenter from outside who was, more or less, agreeable, on one condition. In effect he said:

'Look, what I am doing is at great risk. I shall have to risk the displeasure of local artisans, and probably my position in my own village may also become difficult. Now I cannot run such a great risk unless there is something reasonably worthwhile in it. I shall offer my services if you agree to this condition. You must give me my grain payment in advance. You should fill up a special pit to store this grain. Then you must provide me with a free house. These are my minimum demands. And if you do not concede them I cannot undertake to serve you.'

The farmers found the conditions unacceptable, and accordingly the negotiations broke down. Then the farmers resorted to more questionable methods. They split a carpenter family, by tempting one of them to break away from the rest. But one man proved inadequate for all the farmers. Again the tension went below the surface. After 2 or 3 months' hectic activity, one Lingayat blacksmith succeeded in getting from his *Ayadakulas* the quantum of grain he demanded. But his success was short-lived, and in no time he became unpopular, lost his customers and the good will of the community. An interesting side-incident relates to a farmer who threatened to become his own carpenter. In fact, he did do carpentry on his own. The village soon ridiculed and censured him by conferring on him the nickname 'carpenter'. Thus he lost his 'status' in the eyes of the village. The most significant thing to note is that the whole conflict just petered out, though it was remembered. Five years later, the conflict exploded in connection with the issue of building the ceremonial chariot of Dyamavva.

Another rather serious incident involving the farmers and the carpenters which took place a year ago merits attention. In Shivapur the goddess Dyamavva, a goddess of the carpenters, is considered important for the farmers. She is believed to protect the lands. Hence the farmers are expected to give her gifts during the sowing season. Now, the image of the goddess is in the charge of a carpenter family. Once it so happened that it was in the possession of a comparatively younger member of the carpenter family in question. The farmers forcibly grabbed the image from the young carpenter. Thereupon the leader of the carpenters threw a direct challenge. He got hold of a stick and led his men to the temple of the goddess. At the gate he posted himself and shouted, 'If the goddess is to be carried by you into her temple, this can occur only after we fight you. You can walk over our dead bodies!' The challenge was fortunately not answered. The farmers gave in. The carpenters registered a victory. What would have exploded into a bloody fight was averted by the apparent giving in by one of the parties. I say 'apparent', because in the village such incidents are not easily forgotten, and they may, in different contexts, explode into conflicts.

Then we have the case of a Chikkamath priest who was marked as negligent by a householder. During the festival days the priest is in great demand, and he was called upon to go round officiating in several houses. There is bound to be delay in attending some families. This Chikkamath priest was also handicapped as he was a cripple. He was unable to attend one of the families he was required to attend. The farmer in question resented this and broke his relations with the priest.

On another occasion a Mathapati sent a neighbour to go to the farmer and collect the *Aya* on his behalf. This was taken as an insult by the farmer. He sent word saying that the Mathapati should go himself personally. The Mathapati took offence at this, and thus their relations were broken.

A carpenter had a grudge against his *Ayadakula*. The farmer used to park his bullock-cart in a vacant lot next to his house. The carpenter indicated his resentment, but the farmer persisted. The carpenter built a small shed on the spot, and thus the farmer was unable to make use of it. A conflict broke out, leading to tension between the *Ayagara* and the *Ayadakula*.

An *Ayadakula* demanded that his *Ayagara* blacksmith make what the blacksmith thought an unreasonably large number of sickles. The blacksmith got enraged and asked the farmer, 'Do you go about distributing these sickles among your relatives?' The farmer took offence, and tension resulted between the two.

In the village there is a practice according to which a washerman/washerwoman must be given as a gift the saree that a girl wears at the time of her first menstruation. In one case the *Ayadakula* gave another, a cheaper and older saree. The washerman who came to know of it did not show his resentment openly. He was biding his time. When another daughter had her first menstruation, the farmer tried to repeat his earlier performance, but now the washerman told him bluntly that he would not serve him any longer.

A barber was asked by a person who lived next door to him to go to his place and serve him. The barber requested him to have his hair cut in the place where he was already busy doing the work. The *Ayadakula* took offence at such a request, and this led to tension between the two.

A Korava musician had been booked by parties in a number of surrounding villages during the wedding season. Thus his hands were full. When a local client asked for his services, he was unable to accept. This was resented by the Party, and this again led to strained relations.

Historically, there is the case of the Cheluvadis who refused to do leather-work. There used to be a custom by which the village accountant (Kulkarni) collected three Paise out of every Rupee given as land revenue. The special amount so collected was given to the sweepers, that is, the Cheluvadis. The custom was suddenly discontinued, and the Cheluvadis took the matter to higher officials like the Collector. Thereupon the village agreed to continue the practice. But there was a deliberate delay in implementing the decision. In the meantime the Cheluvadis expressed their resentment by abandoning leather-work and sweeping roads in the village, while one family retained its *Aya* obligations. To this incident people trace the reason why the Cheluvadis do not do leather-work, etc. Three members found jobs in Dhawar Municipality as sweepers, two on the Railways.

A Madiga is traditionally expected to offer a pair of shoes at the time of the marriage of a son or a daughter of his *Ayadakula*. On one occasion the Madiga was unable to offer them. This was sufficient ground for a breakdown in their relations.

3

Society is living together, and as such it cannot carry on without a sharing of minimum common values. The function of generating and preserving such common values needs a special mechanism of its own. It is the basic function of such a mechanism to maintain stable social relations on the basis of common values and to restore balance between social forces. It prescribes the limits beyond which social relations cannot break down. When an abnormal situation is apprehended, the society in Shivapur becomes suddenly cautious. It will avoid taking decisions and performing actions which might lead to the breaking out of such a crisis. Everybody is cautious because everybody is afraid of being the cause of trouble. There is a strong feeling that one should avoid trouble serious enough to disrupt society, and nobody wants to be the cause of such disruption. Hence when a crisis is apprehended, all the parties slow down. Moreover the process of opinion mobilisation is slow. This is a major manner in which extreme situations threatening social orders are averted in Shivapur.

We have seen how quarrels may arise out of personal, ritual and economic factors. But such quarrels are generally given a personal complexion. They are put on a personal level, and thus reduced to a more manageable form of conflict. People come to look upon them as family quarrels. A washerman who was having some trouble with his *Aya-dakula* told us that their quarrel was a *family quarrel*. The point of interest here is that the parties do not see themselves in the roles of buyers and sellers, but as members of a common family. This is in itself a factor tending towards harmony. All alliances and conflicts are thus turned into familial patterns, and are less individualistically conceived. Thus familism is inherent in the *Aya* system.

It is true that the village life is characterised by lack of opportunities, but this should not be mistaken for helplessness. Whatever may be the feelings of an outsider in the matter, the people themselves do not feel that way. Their intense belief in *Karma*, involving re-birth, steels them against all kinds of adversities, and they accept everything, good and bad, with an almost stoic indifference. This spirit of acceptance may be seen both during normal times and in times of stress and strain. However, it would be a grave error if one were to take this as a merely passive attitude. This stoic acceptance of what happens is backed by a system of action in which the idea of retaliation dominates. Even the smallest man at the bottom of the social scale, the untouchable, has scope to retaliate against the highest man at the top, the *Ayadakula*. This possibility of retaliation and the consequent lowering of social prestige that may attend it keeps everyone, high and low, alert and makes for caution. This strengthens the forces of social harmony and balance, and helps keep the ship of society on an even keel. If services are withheld, payments are automatically withheld, and vice versa. If you give less, you get less, whether for giving more you get more or not!

The caste unity and solidarity are also factors which tend to stabilise the social relations. But caste solidarity should not be mistaken for the modern spirit of trade unionism—it is the unity of a total way of living, not simply of professional or economic interests. Each caste is sustained by a group mystique whose ultimate roots are cosmological and metaphysical. It implies the principle that people in good times and bad should co-operate with each other. Caste is, in a sense, a paradoxical institution which is characterised by both inclusive and exclusive tendencies. This feature of caste comes out clearly in the case of the untouchables. While obviously they are excluded systematically from the total system, they are also drawn into it in innumerable ritualistic, economic and political contexts.

The inequalities between *Ayagaras* created by the disparities in the number of *Ayadakulas* each gets is also levelled down in the course of time, since every successive generation splits its inheritance of *Ayadakulas*.

Economic tensions are minimised by the availability of additional work both within and outside the village. When a farmer is in need of extra service he gets it from outside the village, and when a carpenter needs extra income he can get it by doing work in other villages. This goes a long way towards relieving tensions. But getting additional employment outside the village is not without its disadvantages. A few cases may be cited. The son of the local oil-grinder went out of the village to work as a milkman, at Hubli. But the father does not know where he is or what he is doing at the moment. The son of an old barber is also working outside the village as a milkman, and has left his poor old parents unhappy. His old mother earns as a labourer and his father still serves a few old persons in the village. Physical distances tend to sever human links with the village, since those who go out cherish new values conflicting with those of the stay-at-homes. As a result, the local families have tended to minimise such situations. Among them there is a strong reluctance to allow members of their family to leave the village. This has the incidental consequence of limiting labour mobility of the village.

The conflicts and tensions are smoothed over through the operation of the institutions of kinship and marriage. Individual conflicts are settled through their mediation, and thus one kind of conflict is reduced considerably.

Though the egalitarian ideas of the new government tend to come into conflict with the traditional village values, and have weakened traditional institutions like the caste council, the traditional system has enough power to absorb the new values while not surrendering older values entirely. There is adjustment, and the old and the new are wedded into a reasonable compromise. The most outstanding example in this connection is caste. Caste is adjusting itself to the new situation, but without giving up its *essential* functions. It continues to function effectively but in a different context.

The flexibility and resilience of the social system may be seen again in the manner in which the *Aya* has been changed into *Alategalu* in response to changing economic conditions. But again, *Aya* is not discarded and is allowed to coexist in the company of the *Alategalu*. This is another instance of social absorption capable of holding in balance contending forces.

Above all, ultimately and essentially, the main foundation of *Dharma* remains intact. It has proved to be capable of adjusting to changing situations. The sanction behind it is neither law nor police, but some intuitive feeling of what is right and appropriate. If the situation takes an abnormal turn, the *Dharma* intervenes, and normality is restored. The even rhythm of the social pulse is automatically maintained. Thus one sees how the *Aya* system meets successfully the manifold conflicts and tensions that beset it.

VII

THE CHANGING SCENE

I

BEFORE WE GIVE an account of the changes that have come over Shivapur society and explain their causes, a brief recapitulation of the traditional situation is called for. The concept of the village community as a closed and self-sufficient system is now no longer acceptable. In Shivapur, for instance, there are clear inter-village relationships of various kinds and considerable outward mobility. These may be seen in marital relations, in the organisation of festivals, and in the movement of specialists crossing the village territorial limits in both directions. While this was already the position before the advent of national freedom in 1947, the post-Independence years have been characterised by increasing contacts with the outside world.

Four years ago Shivapur was given a railway station of its own and at about the same time a post office was installed in the village. Three years ago the first bus came to the village, whereas earlier the buses had only passed at some distance from the village. But the most momentous development is the contemplated inclusion of Shivapur under the newly formed Hubli-Dharwar Corporation. The people of Shivapur are aware of it and they have sensed the possibility that land prices will shoot up. In the nearby town of Dharwar, the Radio Station (a central government agency) was set up about 16 years ago, thus bringing Shivapur nearer to the outside world. All this, naturally, has had its impact upon the traditional order. The traditional social order has been modified, but only slightly.

This look at the changing scene will focus on the following important areas: caste, economy, politics, and religion. The traditional social structure is profoundly conservative and custom-bound. Even so, it has been forced by circumstances to come to terms with the challenges of the modern world. Our study has broadly shown that the changes made in response to this challenge have been minor adjustments relating to *non-essentials*, and that the basic structure is still very much intact. Change has been accepted, but not to the extent of undermining the traditional foundation. Thus there is a core of continuity around which minor changes have crystallised. We shall examine these areas for the changes that have taken place in them.

Caste: This is an institution based on birth, hierarchy, endogamy and occupation. It is also characterised by rules of purity and pollution. So far as the principle of birth goes, there has been no change. One's position in the caste system is determined by birth. There have, however, been five cases of conversion, but significantly they were to the Muslim faith, and for marriage reasons. So birth must be reckoned as a permanent, unchanging element of caste.

The principle of hierarchy has not disappeared. On the contrary, it is very much in evidence. The traditional hierarchical pattern is going strong, and our study has failed to discover the emergence of a new economic class to which some writers make reference. The hierarchy is still caste-bound. Though modified legally or constitutionally, the hierarchical pattern dominates in the new contexts as well. In the tea-shops, there is a degree of equality in the sense that all may enter, but the older pattern may be detected in the fact that the untouchables have to squat on the floor, avoid the bench or raised platform, drink from cups especially set apart for them, and themselves clean the cups after drinking the tea. In the schools, the children mix freely, and yet they do not eat or drink together, and when they return home the high-caste children take a ritual wash.

The occupations are, as before, arranged hierarchically. In the Panchayat meetings, the seating arrangements are such as to bring the members of higher castes nearer the dais. The houses are also so arranged that those belonging to the higher castes are nearer to the centre of the village while those of the untouchables are on the periphery. Thus one sees in this aspect some small changes, but the basic idea remains as strong as ever.

Endogamous rules have changed, if at all, only on a negligible scale. The system of arranged marriages, which is one of the main means of preserving the rules of endogamy, is very prevalent. A marriage is regarded, primarily, as a matter between family and family, and lineage and lineage, but not between individuals. Love marriage is non-existent. A boy, more often than not, marries a girl whom he has never seen at all or only hastily during the engagement ceremony. As for the girl, she would not have had the boldness to raise her eyes to look at her future husband. The dominant factors in the settlement of a marriage are still property, caste and kinship status.

Caste is still identifiable with occupational specialisation. No doubt individual mobility of an artisan in spatial terms has increased, but there is little or no mobility between occupations. Individual members of a particular occupation may move out of the village in order to earn a little extra, but that is all. Some rare instances of persons taking to other secondary occupations are noticeable, but the important point is that the primary, traditional occupation is seldom abandoned. When the primary occupation is abandoned, both the community and the person concerned regard it as something wrong, against *Dharma*. We have mentioned a Chikkamath priest who also practices as a medical man. In short, minor adjustments may be made to meet temporary economic needs, but essentially the traditional occupation to which one is born dominates. Thus no *essential* changes are noticeable in this aspect.

Social distance is still largely observed in Shivapur, though changes can be seen in some respects. Localities are still arranged along caste lines. As the total area of the village has not changed much, the arrangement of streets, also on caste lines, illustrates dramatically the dominance of the caste system in the village. Streets here are known as the weaver street, the washerman street, the untouchable street, etc. Yet one should beware of overemphasising this point, for there are factors which make for the unity of the village community as a whole.

We may summarise the changes that have been initiated in the caste system in Shivapur in recent times. Thirty years ago it was inconceivable that one could drink water touched by a sub-caste member. Now the rules of commensality have been relaxed and inter-dining is permitted within a single caste. The tea-shop has been a real leveller in this respect. This is one kind of change. Secondly, there is a clear tendency to underplay or discard the *non-essential* details of a ritual, without the ritual itself being rejected. Thus one can perceive that the older, traditional attitudes and values are very much holding their ground. Thirdly, children of different castes mix under such auspices as the new school. Here again there is no *essential* change. Children may sit in the same class, but they do not eat or drink what is touched by children of other castes; and when they go home they take a ritual wash. Fourthly, the rules of pollution and purity regarding food have been relaxed owing to the introduction of modern transport. In the olden days the bullock-cart was the only means of transport, and one could carry one's food in it without having it polluted. But in a bus or train such a luxury is unthinkable. Fifthly, the practice of sitting equally in a modern bus has helped to break untouchability. But this is nothing new, since even in earlier days untouchability was relaxed during public occasions like village festivals. One can see that the change in this respect is not very deep.

Economy: Though farming is the main occupation in Shivapur, it is by no means the only important occupation. It must be borne in mind that about 40 per cent of the population are not directly involved in farming. As in a modern economy, there is here a variety of occupational specialisations. However, this is more rigid than in the modern economy. The occupation of farming is denied to all castes from the Marathas down to the untouchables, because of land scarcity. The new tenancy laws have contributed to the break-up of land concentration. The occupational structure is essentially rigid, and such mobility as exists is negligible. It is difficult for an individual to move up the economic scale. This has been one of the reasons for the rigidity of the system. It is interesting to note that as a result of the new tenancy laws involving the abolition of absentee landlordism, a whole street of landlords called the Desai street, ('Desai' means landlord) has been deserted by the Desais. This is also symbolic of the fact that the concentration of land has been seriously disturbed.

The economy of Shivapur, presupposes a close functional interdependence of various groups. Even the proximity of an agricultural college and a thick cluster of higher educational institutions has hardly disturbed the position in this regard. The traditional interdependence is a basic fact.

This is a highly intimate economy in which economic transactions depend more upon personal services and obligations than upon cash incentives. The bank, for instance, is foreign to the spirit of such an economy. The methods of production are not geared to a cash economy, and the monumental failure of a tractor, of which more will be said later, is an indication of the degree to which the local economy has rejected modern methods of production. The tools and implements employed are largely traditional and primitive.

Such changes as have been introduced have been negligible. For example, the plough has been changed only to the extent that a new piece of iron is tagged on to it at its furrowing end. Practically all tools and implements are old-fashioned and produced in the traditional style by the local artisans.

If this is the situation regarding production, the exchange system of the economy is equally predominantly traditional. Production of goods is not considered as a merely economic, market-oriented process with monetary motives, but is regarded as a way of life. Grain is the currency in so far as it is the dominant material exchanged between parties involved in the countless exchange transactions. Cattle are still regarded as a most important investment. Though barter prevails, the predominant pattern is the more complex system of exchange of gifts such as grain, services and tools. These exchanges characterise a person's life from birth to death.

Now let us look in detail at the changes that have been attempted with such success as they may actually be said to have been achieved. An important institution in this respect is the co-operative. There are in Shivapur two co-operative societies which may be designed co-operative no. 1 and no. 2. No. 1 co-operative society is a half-century old; and no. 2, a newcomer, was introduced 16 years ago. The story of the co-operative is pertinent and bears detailed narration. One of the chairmen of co-operative no. 1 took it into his head to amass property for the co-operative, and actually acquired for it property worth about Rs. 40,000. But the methods he had employed in getting it were considered to be irregular by the higher co-operative officials, who were applying the rules rigidly. It was not permissible for a co-operative to indulge in real estate business or oil-grinding enterprises, however profitable. These official strictures dampened the local enthusiasm for the co-operative, and co-operative no. 1 has now become merely a loaning bank, borrowing funds from the district authorities and lending them to villagers at the prescribed interest. This co-operative has become a high-caste affair, dominated by the upper-class farmers.

Co-operative no. 2 was started 16 years ago by the lower groups and is dominated by the labourers. A Lingayat priest with very dubious antecedents managed to become secretary. This man had been earlier dismissed from his position as a clerk in the Revenue Department. He got his opportunity to make some money when the District co-operative, for questionable reasons, took a keen interest in selling tractors. The Chairman of the District co-operative was not so much interested in improving agriculture as in helping a friend in the tractor business. The village bank was offered loans for the purchase of a tractor. Shivapur bought tractor, not so much because it wanted one as because loans could be raised on the security of the tractor.

The idea was to hire out the tractor and to repay the loan with the money thus obtained. However, the tractor was hired out arbitrarily and the rental was not collected properly. The Chairman's son was one of the few to get a clear benefit out of the whole business since he was employed to manage the tractor. A further round of loans was offered to the villagers to enable them to clear off the earlier loan taken for the purchase of the tractor. The tractor, in the meanwhile, was allowed to rust, and the whole venture came to nothing. The labourers became involved in heavy debts. The village community, which regarded the tractor as a symbol of the new values, felt unhappy about it, and rejected it.

Regarding the traditional *Aya* system, there has been change in so far as the unmeasured *Aya* is now supplemented by the measured *Alategalu* (measured grain). But *Aya* is still very important. The farmer's reliance upon the carpenter and the blacksmith is increasingly due to more production and the uncertainty posed by the failure of the tractor. Then the increased cost of living has prompted the villagers to supplement their traditional income by working for cash. Lastly, the farmers have now taken to growing cash crops, and this is a change of considerable importance. Production has gone up because of the use of fertilisers, and this has stimulated the economy generally. However, it should be noted that most of these changes are not new and have been at work for a considerable time. What is new is that now the pace of change has increased perceptibly.

Politics and Administration: Before independence there did exist contacts between the representatives of the government and the villagers. But the officers were considered as outsiders, symbols of the urban world. The officers used to visit the village for the purpose of supervision or collection of taxes, etc. With the advent of independence, such contacts have become more frequent. The subsequent reorganisation of states in 1956 has not brought the state closer to the lives of the villagers, since the new capital, Bangalore, is as far away as the old capital, Bombay. However, there is a difference, because the new goverment is headed by people who speak the same language as that spoken by the Shivapur villagers. To this extent the government has been able to achieve a greater emotional identification with the people. Apart from this, the bureaucratic structure remains as alien to them as before. The operation of the governmental agencies is regarded as no real concern of theirs. Its unimaginative attitude has increased this sense of estrangement. An interesting episode comes to mind in this connection. The village has a tank. The tank bred fish. The villagers wanted to auction the fish. Then the local Panchayat tomtomed (the traditional announcement in public through a drummer) that the State Department of Fisheries would auction the fish. People resented this, as they thought an outside agency was trying to make money out of what belonged to them. Before the day the auction took place people organised themselves and collected a substantial portion of the fish, and the government officials were kept fully ignorant of this event.

The important thing to note is that in the eyes of the village, the Panchayat is identified with the state. Such an attitude has turned the villagers away from modern political institutions and led them to seek leadership in the traditional caste council as against the Panchayat council. The institution of election is not new, and the police were also there before independence, so that the village does not feel a marked difference between pre- and post-Independence times so far as they are concerned. There are two kinds of political leadership in the village, one traditional and the other new. The leaders of the caste council belong to the former category, having acquired this status largely by heredity, and they represent more faithfully the local opinion. They are not elected, whereas the new leadership in the Panchayat is elective but not really as effective as its traditional counterpart.

This brings us to the changes that have been effected in the political situation. The greatest single change has been the new democratically constituted statutory Panchayat. This institution has formally replaced the caste council. The caste council has been reduced to virtual impotence since it has been legally divested of its power to excommmicate. Elections have been introduced on a larger scale, too. The ballot method is also new. Although these look like sweeping changes, it must be admitted that they have hardly touched the fundamental social structure. Though caste has apparently been reduced in importance, it has gained new strength under the new dispensation. The new Panchayat has brought in the new egalitarian ideology, but only outwardly. The representatives of women and untouchables in the Panchayat are simply there because the new law requires it. They are mere dummies that never attend the Panchayat meetings. Thus we can see that the change is not deep. As a matter of fact, all these changes have been made to serve conservative tendencies, and have reinforced the basic institutions of the traditional order—caste and kinship.

The idea of political parties is a novel one. In the earlier days one could easily align one's loyalties with one's caste and kinship groups, but now the villager is called upon to produce a new kind of loyalty to a political party. The villagers have shown a considerable awareness of the national political parties, but this has to be carefully distinguished from the fact that such awareness has had little impact on voting behaviour. Voting continues to be along caste and kinship lines. In the last general election in 1962, we noticed that the Panchayat chairman was canvassing for the Indian National Congress party, while two other members of the Panchayat were canvassing for the P.S.P. (Praja Socialist Party) and the Jan Sangh Party. The presence of the police during the election was considered normal. Women showed practically no political awareness, since they were herded into caste groups and taken to the polling booth to cast their votes. Most of them voted Congress, since the Congress symbol, a pair of bullocks, was closer to their life.

The introduction of the statutory Panchayat has brought about a fission between the caste leaders and the various new political leaders. It is clear that the caste leaders are more powerful and, in all important decisions of the Panchayat, they have a decisive hand. It is they, not the new political leaders, who took a crucial role in the settlement of the conflict between the farmers and the artisans of Shivapur. Usually these traditional leaders take no formal part in the proceedings of the Panchayat, but in times of crisis it is to them that the Panchayat turns. However, the new political offices have brought new values, and some of these values have become gradually associated with youth. The older generation is associated with the older caste values. Thus one can see a more than normal conflict of generations. The overall impression is that new values, new institutions and new leaders are emerging, but the older order continues to have the upper hand.

Ritual and Religion: In this area again, only very slight changes are noticeable. The Hindus and Muslims have their traditional festivals and rituals, and each caste has its own set of rites and festivals. These are flourishing as rigorously as before, though with slight modifications. The ritual norms of religious and cast groups are largely intact. The *Basavajayanti* and the *Moharrum*, which are observed by the whole village, are still popular. The purity and pollution rules may be slightly altered, but they are far from being discarded. The ruling religious and ethical values continue to be *Karma* (one's efforts in this or other births) and *Dharma* (duty in accordance with one's essential nature).

The changes that have affected this area may now be described. While old religious festivals continue, some newer ones have come. To the traditional Hindu pantheon have now been added secular gods like Gandhi and Nehru, in the case of all; Shivaji in the case of the Marathas, and Jinnah, in the case of the Muslims. In addition to the traditional ritual calendar, the secular calendar also is consulted. The radio, for instance, at the beginning of its news bulletins announces the date both according to the traditional Hindu calendar and according to the modern calendar. There has been some relaxation in the ritual rules in certain contexts. Younger people nowadays do not always bathe after a shave.

Material Culture: With regard to dress, hair style and ornaments, one notes a similar co-existence of the old and the new. Dress reflects social differentiations on the basis of caste, sex and age qualifications. During infancy, a male child has an embroidered cap and an embroidered shirt. A baby girl wears a cowl-like head dress. Younger men wear the dhoti, a turban on the head and a shirt without cuffs or collar. The older men wear a dhoti, a shirt without buttons and fastened with strings (called *Kise Angi*), and a turban. Young girls before puberty wear a coloured saree and a blouse. Older women also wear a coloured saree and a blouse. In both cases the sarees are generally produced by the local weavers. There have been observable changes in this respect. Formerly all dress material was wholly of local make. But nowadays the local weaver is being replaced increasingly by the mills outside. The local weaver processes the mill-made yarn to make local sarees. The locally produced saree represents the older values, and yet it is being adopted as the latest fashion by the women who are the last word in fashion—the Bombay film stars. Thus it has come about that the local saree is even exported to Bombay.

The increasing use of the mill cloth must be attributed to its cheapness, variety and ready availability. You can just go to a shop and pick it up. This should not be taken to mean that the home-spun saree has been elbowed out entirely. It has its honoured place. As for the dress of men, the buttonless string-fastened shirt has almost totally disappeared, and we could discover only five persons above 50 years old using it. Among the younger generation, the turban has been replaced by the cap. The local dhoti with a red border has now been discontinued except during ceremonial occasions, and the mill dhoti has taken its place. Among the young women, the mill-made saree has pushed out the local saree. For instance, it was invariably our experience that school girls wore the imported factory saree whereas married women used the indigenous product.

Of the traditional ornaments, the ear-rings, the nose-rings, the bangles and the *Tali* (the wedding necklace) are still prevalent. All other ornaments which used to burden the bodies of womenfolk have almost vanished. Women of bygone ages could be seen heavily laden with ornaments of all sizes, designs and weights, covering their bodies from head to toe! A new kind of ornament is the necklace. The new gold control rules prohibiting the manufacture of ornaments of more than 14 carat gold have virtually thrown the village goldsmith out of a job, since his tools are not equal to the task of making ornaments of less than 14 carat gold. Thus the mass-produced new gold ornaments from urban places are flooding the local market. Among men the only ornaments to be seen are cuff-links or watches, which are made of gold. The difficulty of getting gold ornaments has naturally increased the demand for silver ornaments.

Traditionally both older men and younger men had their heads shaved. Now the style is the crop. The younger people of the village who go to schools or colleges find it necessary to go to the salons in Dharwar. Women's hair-style has shown practically no change whatsoever.

So far as domestic utensils are concerned, old pots and pans have been replaced to a small extent. The potter and his ware are now considered necessary mostly for ritual occasions, for instance, during weddings. In place of these old articles, utensils made of German silver, aluminium and stainless steel are now used. Stainless steel is still a luxury, however, and we could find only three or four farmer families using it.

In all the above studies, we have seen that older patterns and habits have not been completely jettisoned, while new ones are also accepted. However, the significant fact is that the changes are accepted generally and invariably with regard to what may be called *non-essential* aspects. Basically the old dominates.

2

In this section we shall map the changes that have been effected group-wise, and with the use of relevant case studies.

Farmer: The older farmers whom we contacted told us that they had witnessed many changes in their lifetime, with respect to the family, religion, economy, politics and law. So far as the family is concerned, one notices a greater amount of education being given to the children. While very few parents were literate, they almost always had children at school. In the school itself, the teacher has changed his methods. The older 'spare the rod and spoil the child' type no longer functions. This has had an important effect on the behavioural pattern of the family. The head of the family has now become less authoritarian than he used to be.

The school-going children must be counted among the most important agents of change.

In the case of marriage, the farmers say that some change has occurred. Formerly the arranged marriage ruled out the chance of a boy seeing a girl before marriage. Nowadays young men want to see the girl at least during the engagement ceremony. The joint family is still dominant, and a survey we made confirmed our impression that an overwhelming majority of the people in Shivapur want it to continue. So far as the marriage ceremony goes, there is a remarkable reduction in duration. In the olden days, a marriage was a prolonged affair lasting one full week. It was an occasion when every member of the large extended family turned up. It involved elaborate rituals, some of which concerned the family hearth and the family deities.

Today all this has gone. A marriage at best lasts for three days. It is usually held in a temple, and it has been nicknamed the 'Congress marriage', presumably because it has been a product of Congress Raj! Or it may be because it is economic and modern. In a public temple, there is no scope for performing such ceremonies as worshipping the family hearth and the family gods. Thus the ritualistic aspect has declined appreciably. As far as the kinship situation is concerned, there has been change. Now the kinship ties and loyalties have extended beyond the territorial limits of the village, and political support is canvassed in a much wider territorial context.

In the economic sphere, the good old bullock is still king. The modern railway and the automobile have not disturbed his supremacy. The upper-class farmers now use fertilisers and better seeds. The cash crops such as fruits have now become common. The villagers have come to use the compost-pits for manuring. Among the cash crops, grapes are an innovation. The traditional economic relations between the farmer and the middle castes like the artisans have not changed, but those between the farmers and the lowest caste, i.e. untouchables, have altered. Some farmers no longer buy their leather goods from the Cheluvadis, but get them from the outside market. The interesting thing is that the Cheluvadis also buy them from the market and give them to the farmers whenever a customary or traditional context requires it.

In the field of politics, there is now the new leadership of the statutory Panchayat based on elections. The traditional leadership of the caste councils not only continues, however, but dominates politically. But the elections have now introduced a new value; that of competition and contest as well as of popular consent, as against the older one of birth. The new political institutions have brought in new status values, and sex and caste equality.

The Priest: Traditionally the priest was required to perform ritual bathing and worshipping on all Mondays and ritual days. This was known as *madi* and *udi* (ritual cleanliness and ritual dress). This is declining now. Inter-dining and inter-drinking between sub-castes have now become totally accepted. Formerly the traditional payments to the priest were not measured, but now they are. The *Ulipi*, for instance, is now measured.

The traditional wedding pattern with its many rites and ceremonies, starting with the bride-search and ending with the nuptial consummation, could not but involve the priest at every stage. But the new 'Congress' marriage, which is of a much shorter duration and is far less elaborate ritualistically, has reduced the role of the priest substantially. The *Guggala*, a religious ceremony during a wedding, has now become rare. This was considered a prestige ceremony.

Formerly the Linayats regularly had the Hiremath and Chikkamath priests worship their house gods and then eat with them, on Mondays and Fridays. But now only 5 families are known to do this. However, it is done on important ceremonial occasions by all. Among the Marathas such weekly visits of the priest have also disappeared, and only one family is known to continue the practice.

The Changing Scene

There is little change to record with regard to the minor priests like the Mathapati, Ganachari and Hugar.

The Goldsmith: 50 years ago the bodies of the farmer women weighed heavily with gold. Now gold has become scarce, and it is anybody's guess where it has gone. Heavy ornaments have been replaced by the lighter ones, and men now wear no ornaments proper. Meanwhile the goldsmith's mobility has increased owing to modern transport, while the factory has reduced his importance as a producer of ornaments. His magical role has been reduced because of the modern medical and hygienic facilities. The decreased use of ornaments has also meant a decline in the ritual status of the goldsmith. Both the occasion of placing an order for ornaments and the occasion of receiving them from the goldsmith involved elaborate ceremonies to which we have already referred. Now the ornaments have become secularised. The new gold control rules have taken the bread out of the mouth of the goldsmith. He is in danger of becoming extinct as an occupational specialist. All this will disturb not only the goldsmith's own position in the social system, but also his role as an indicator, via the ornaments he made, of social differentiations. One may say that the goldsmith has suffered a severe structural dislocation. Of the 5 goldsmith families in Shivapur, 2 have completely given up the occupation and the others are preparing to. However, one goldsmith boy, Manohar, overcome by pride in the traditional craft of his ancestors, declared that he would keep at least one of his brothers in the traditional family occupation.

The Potter: Shivapur has no potter of its own. But the potter's services are ritualistically important, and outside help is sought. The introduction of metal utensils has reduced his secular importance. People have now taken to German silver and aluminium, and more rarely to stainless steel.

The Changing Scene

The Carpenter: The Carpenters we interviewed complained that the work-load has increased, and this is due to increased production. Both farmers, i.e. *Ayadakulas,* and carpenters, i.e. *Ayagaras,* are aware of it. One of the reasons for the increase in work-load is the cash motive. The farmers want more money and so they increase production. This automatically adds to the work of the artisans like the carpenter. Thus he asks for more, and not merely more, but for a measured quantum of grain from the farmer. This is how the *Alategalu* (measured grain) has been introduced. But *Alategalu* has not replaced the older *Ayadakalu* (the unmeasured grain). The carpenter is forced to make both ends meet by making non-traditional earnings. He does it outside the village, and inside he gets extra remuneration for building work. The local red-tiled buildings of the school and the Panchayat are an index of his additional income. Another interesting change has been the innovation of *Teneganike* (the gift of the top grains) at harvest time. One notes also that the relations between *Ayadakula* and *Ayagara* are now more formal. But this is a merely verbal, surface phenomenon, and the traditional relations are as strong as ever.

The Blacksmith: Today iron implements are available in the outside market, and iron is a commodity whose sale is controlled by the government. Iron is a metal which is used in almost every aspect of local life. Improved methods of production involve more implements and thus more iron has to be used. This has increased the blacksmith's work-load greatly. One Shivapur blacksmith demanded *Alategalu* and got it. This blacksmith has two children both specialising in smithy work at a technical school. This is a case of the link between the old and the new.

The Washerman: Apart from his traditional work under the *Aya* system, he is hired by the laundries in Dharwar, for which he gets extra income. Also his traditional service includes only *nir madi* (merely washing in water), and ironing has to be paid extra. Two of the local washermen have opened laundries in Dharwar and have become carriers of new values and ways to the village. In the town, work is more organised, since timings are fixed. This has made Shivapur washermen think along new lines. They also have seen that in the town the washerman is treated on a level of equality with everyone else. Yet no local washerman is prepared to give up his traditional work.

The Barikar: This has been one of the most changed groups so far as functions go. In the olden days, they functioned as village servants. They served the temples, lit the village street-lights and the temple lights, and generally attended to village public work. Now the coming of the new Panchayat has meant the emergence of new paid officials who perform the functions which used to be done by the Barikars. They have been, so to say, uprooted functionally, having nothing to do with the new Panchayat. Formerly they used to be of service at marriages, when they would wash the utensils or attend to guests' cattle. But the fact that the 'Congress' marriages are the fashion has reduced their work considerably in this respect, too.

The Korava: In the traditional pattern of the Korava life one notes an important change. The traditional style of music of the Korava is played through the *Shehnai* (a small, doleful pipe). The new band music has upset the traditional pattern. The band music has acquired prestige in the village. As a result the Koravas have now bought a set of band instruments, and play them. However, their traditional music has not died out completely.

The Ganiga: The oil-presser, the Ganiga, has vanished out of Shivapur life. People buy their oil from the nearby urban centre. Hand-pressed oil has been replaced by kerosene.

There does not seem to be any possibility of the function being revived in Shivapur.

The Barber: The pattern of the barber's activities also reveals a combination of old and new traits. There is his usual traditional service for the *Ayadakula*. In addition, he does extra work for cash payment. Thus we can see both the gift economy and the cash economy involved in his work. There is one salon in Shivapur, and a local barber has set up a salon in Dharwar. As in the case of the washerman, this has led to the introduction of new, urban values in the village. The local primary school teacher and a few college-going youths have taken to the safety razor. In consequence, the notion of pollution associated with barber's services has undergone a change. Those who shave themselves do not deem it necessary to take a ritual bath. The tonsure ceremony, which involves the barber in a ritualistic aspect, continues to be practised. A barber's son sells milk in Dharwar, and this has led to a break with his family life in the village.

The Untouchable: A most remarkable aspect of the changes introduced in an attempt to improve his status is that all such attempts have gone against him. For example, the Panchayat gives him equal representation, and his very vote has made him vulnerable. One Madiga was threatened by his *Ayadakula* that he would 'take care of him' if he did not vote for him. At the risk of incurring the displeasure of his *Ayadakula*, he voted for a popular Maratha leader. Thus the Madigas have come to regard the privilege of voting as more trouble than it is actually worth. They feel that people go to them for votes during elections, and thereafter do nothing for them. The leather goods from the town market have reduced their work. Poverty and lack of work have driven the untouchables to take to manual labour. Thus they feel legitimately that they have lost both their security and their peace.

The Constitution of India states that untouchability is abolished. It promulgates the new ideology of equality. The high-caste Hindus of Shivapur sought to accept this revolutionary idea in their own way. They called the untouchables and told them that if they were to become 'touchable', they must give up eating meat. This promise was made on oath by touching holy water. This incident occurred ten years ago. Since then the Cheluvadis have given up leather-work and the Madigas have been selling skins in Dharwar market. Most of Shivapur's untouchables have gone out as labourers. Though they have acquired the dubious benefit of becoming 'touchables', they feel that they have lost in other respects, both socially and economically. Even the abolition of untouchability itself has not been clearly accepted. As we have pointed out earlier, in the tea-shops the untouchables have to squat on the ground, drink from special cups and wash them after they drink. The Cheluvadis have given up both leather-work and sweeping. The untouchable was, and is, employed to tom-tom, i.e. beat a large drum and make public announcements. Formerly this service was not paid for, but now it is. Our own research investigation was publicised in this way, and the villagers were requested to offer us all help. The untouchable has no status as an *Ayagara*, strictly speaking. Yet he is dependent on an *Ayadakula* and gets gifts throughout the year. Formerly he was called upon to do compulsory work for officers of the village, but now this has gone. The Madigas have been hit hard by the availability of shoes from the urban market. In one curious way they have acquired a new status. This is through the Prayer Meetings (*Bhajana Mandals*), groups of untouchables organised to sing devotional songs. Their services are requisitioned during a death ceremony by special request. This has given them a new socio-religious status.

The Landless Labourer: Formerly there was very little opportunity for him to get employment outside the village. Within the village itself he was subject to seasonal unemployment. Now there is increased production within the village, which needs him, and outside there is any amount of construction work which demands his services. In Dharwar, quite a few of these labourers can be seen working on building projects.

3

We will now turn to the factors and causes which are responsible for the changes discussed above.

State and Government: The Constitution, the rule of law, democracy and secularism, implying individualistic and egalitarian ideals, have created new values. New pro-grammes of socio-economic changes initiated by planning, *Panchayatiraj,* Community Development and the compul-sory primary education, have made the village society open to new forces. Now the villagers are at least aware that outside assistance, in whatever ideological guise, can be got. State-subsidised schemes are now seen to be beneficial locally. Formerly Bombay used to be the capital of State Government, and now it is Bangalore, where the villagers know that their language is spoken. This has tied them closer to the government. Now the district officers and ministers speak to them in their own language, and this has brought the village emotionally closer to the government.

Law: Law is not necessarily an effective vehicle of change, though it could be. In Shivapur law has not been an effective agent of change. For instance, under the law, women have an equal share in property. But, in fact, a woman never gets it, and nobody thinks of going to law. No doubt, the new inheritance and adoption laws, and the tenancy laws, amount to a fundamental socio-economic revolution. Law has taken away the strength of the traditional caste councils. Legally untouchability has gone. Marriage laws have been made to give marriage the status of a contract. Divorce is legally permitted. But all these impressive legal changes have no relation to social realities as seen in Shivapur. Only one woman has sought divorce. Untouchability is practised in a more covert manner. Marriage continues to be regarded as a religious rite. However, changes may come about, perhaps slowly.

Technology: Bicycles, the current craze in Shivapur, buses and the railway have brought the village nearer to the outside world which is, after all, the source of change. To the same outside influence belongs the introduction of the radio. Even as this report is being compiled, we hear that Shivapur is getting electricity. The new technology of the urban centres has solved the water problem of the village, both for drinking and irrigation purposes. The government agencies have controlled pests successfully. The laundry, the salon and the tea-shop have made their appearance. The local barber uses the new hair cutting machine in place of the old razor. Cups and saucers have come with the tea-shops.

Education: Local education is restricted to the proverbial three R's. Yet the children who go to school and the young people who go from schools to colleges are agents of change. The newspaper which is read and the radio which is listened to at the tea-shops are also educational in their own way. The political parties and the government planners, the village level workers, all have been educating the people in the new values and ways.

Universal Suffrage: This institution has been an important equaliser. The traditional non-elective political leadership has been disturbed, even if slightly, by the new elected leadership, whether by show of hands or by casting of votes.

Abolition of Absentee Landlords: The new tenancy laws have abolished the absentee landlord. The tiller is made to feel that he is the owner. This has resulted in the emigration of landlords from the village.

Trade: Local tradesmen, the grocers, the labourers, the salon operator, the tea-shop owners, all these bring into Shivapur life new goods which are associated with new values. This has initiated some change in attitudes. Jaggery has been replaced by sugar from the town. Tea has become a symbol of modernism; it is regarded as fashionable to drink tea. With the tea-shop have arrived cups, saucers, coffee, and biscuits. Other new items are soap, hair-oil, ink-pots and paper. Thus many links with the outside money economy have been forged.

The Panchayat: It has introduced the new egalitarian ideology. The traditional gossip centre has beome more formalised, and the Panchayat is its expression. At the Panchayat meetings, officials have face-to-face contacts with the villagers.

The Co-operative Society: This has been both an agent of change and of conservatism. Borrowing from one's own castemen and kinsmen is now replaced by borrowing from the impersonal society.

The Community Development: This has introduced the ideas of self-help, and has brought into existence youth organisations. It has brought the village closer to modern values and ideals through specially organised fairs, festivals and exhibitions, and has been the most conscious agent of change.

The Health Schemes: The government-sponsored health schemes have also brought in new ideas of human potentialities. Vaccination is now accepted. Malaria has been virtually controlled and plague has disappeared, but the older pattern of behaviour has not been given up. People still go to Dyamavva and Durgavva seeking cures for physical ills. Our investigation showed that about 40 per cent of the people had not taken vaccination against cholera when the disease struck recently. Nevertheless, the proportion that did so represents a considerable vote in favour of modern health schemes.

Famines and Droughts: Famines and droughts still affect human life. Men still depend on nature, but famines and droughts are temporary misfortunes. These have stimulated men to accept ways that they would normally reject.

4

In conclusion, we can say that these changes have been affected mainly by the externals of life. Often they are merely verbal and do not correspond to actual behaviour. Let us briefly examine this observation by taking up our main areas of study one by one.

The Family: The joint family is still dominant, and there is a decisive current of public opinion in favour of it. Its desirability is seen to lie in its security and strength, and in its protective and insurance functions. At the time of our investigation, a carpenter family split. In the division of property that followed, a pair of bullocks got separated. A brother who was attached to the pair got only one as his share. I saw him weep at the prospect of losing one of the pair of bullocks. The break-ups of joint families which have occurred are not the result of mere individualism. The prevalence of the joint family is due partly to the nature of the work involved in agricultural processes, but also to the emotional security it provides. It is interesting that the landless artisans are no less attached to the joint family. The priest still dominates in family life. Arranged marriages are still normal, though now the boy can see the girl at the engagement time. We have not come across a single case of love marriage. In the choice of partners, economic, caste and kinship status are decisive. The authoritarian pattern in the family is still dominant. Elder brothers and grandparents are considered figures of authority in the family.

Economy: Though cash economy has been partially accepted, it has not radically affected the traditional economy. The bullock still dominates the village life. The tractor has failed both as a technological and a moral phenomenon. Reliance on machinery is not deep enough. Traditional methods of production dominate: though a few upper-class farmers have used man-made fertilisers and better seeds, the ordinary farmer still uses cowdung to fertilise his land.

Law: Though the new laws of the government are resorted to whenever necessary, the villagers depend more on the customary law whose ultimate sanction is moral. It is held that going to a court of law is a less dignified act than going to the customary law. In this connection, the importance of the caste council may be noted. This institution has legally lost power, but in reality it is still very powerful.

Religion and Caste: The rules of caste regarding untouchability, pollution and purity are still maintained, though in a more subtle form in order to circumvent the positive law. The new changes have strengthened caste. While older ties of kinship/caste have become looser, the new impersonal ties have yet to become viable. The interdependence of caste upon caste is still strong. The traditional landlord-tenant and master-servant relations have disappeared, to be sure, but the farmer-artisan and the landed-landless relations remain intact. The traditional ideal of giving and receiving survives, and the old pattern of payments is still dominant.

Medicine: The indigenous approach is not rejected, though modern methods are also accepted. For instance, all the children we saw wore a black talisman. The people first consult an astrologer and the local medical man. If they fail to get cured, they rush to the modern hospital. They receive vaccination, and yet they propitiate Dyamavva or Durgavva.

The Changing Scene

The Calendar: Both the ritual calendar and the secular calendar are consulted, but in different contexts. It is interesting that the tea-shops have the secular calendar hanging from their walls. The ritual calendar is more consulted than the secular, which is used only for secular purposes such as office or court work.

The seven types of relations to which we have already made reference are still dominant. All the parties are aware of the new values and ideas from outside. Though the new values may be idealised and appreciated, they are always cast in customary, traditional terms. The traditional life is also idealised. New values, when accepted, are seen as essentially the older values. The ideal of *Dharma* is still important, as is also the *Karma*. When, say, medical help fails, people blame it on their *karma*. I came across a barber whose child, after all Herculean efforts, could not survive. He blamed it on his *karma*.

Society is dynamic, but never to the extent of rejecting the old outright. All changes are shaped to fit into the traditional framework. Rights and privileges in the modern sense are not asserted. But what is important is that they are still maintained, although in terms of *Dharma*. Equality in the modern sense is still foreign to the village, while traditional rights and obligations prevail. One is struck by the remarkable ability of the village community to preserve tradition while accepting change.

One dramatic expression of this pattern of thinking and acting is the way the artisans have preserved their traditional occupation while showing themselves not averse to supplementing their incomes in non-traditional ways. The story of the goldsmith boy, Manohar, who, despite the doom that hangs over his traditional occupation, wants to keep one of his brothers in the goldsmith profession, seems to evidence the tenacity that sustains the Shivapur society in times of crisis and uncertainty.

VIII

EVALUATION

OUR INVESTIGATIONS LEAD us to formulate a sociology of exchange. The Shivapur society is sustained throughout its structure and dynamics by a series of exchange transactions. These involve exchanges of goods and services between individuals and individuals, individuals and groups, groups and groups, groups and the village community as a whole, and between the village and neighbouring villages. This is a traditional society which looks deceptively simple but is actually highly complex and heterogeneous. It is not at all isolated and is related to a larger society. The key term *Aya* explains the exchange aspect of the society. The components of the *Aya* system are not reducible to modern economic, political and legal concepts. To arrive at a proper understanding of the system one needs to take into account the specific local context as well as the context of the larger society to which it is related.

The *Aya* system is a noteworthy institution which belongs to the family of gift systems of which there is a wide variety scattered practically all over the world. The facts and data regarding it have to be looked at as constituting a totality— an integrated and inter-connected social system. The *Aya* system embraces a wide network of social relations, political, legal, religious, economic, and one can scarcely hope to understand it without taking cognizance of both the sum total of its present manifestations and its evolutionary roots in the ancient Indian ideology of *Papa* (sin), *Punya* (merit), *Karma* (destiny) and *Dharma* (duty consonant with one's essential nature).

138

Evaluation

In this welter of gift relationships, the question of who gives and who receives is not only difficult to establish, but is even irrelevant in a sense. The gift complex of the *Aya* involves three crucial elements—giving, receiving and re-paying. One who gives is considered superior to one who does not, irrespective of considerations like caste, age, sex and occupation. Landowning has no special status as such in this approach. A person might own more land, but it does not automatically entitle him to a status of superiority. He who gives more is respectfully known as *Doddakula* (owner of a large number of ploughs and hence *Dodda*, i.e. big), *Hiriya* (elder), *Odeya* (master), and *Yajaman* (master). He who gives more receives more and then repays. The whole social scene is made up of this basically triadic sequence of trans-actions—giving, receiving and repaying—in an endless chain.

If you are given something you must receive, and refusal to do so is taken to mean that either you do not think the gift worth receiving or you think that you cannot repay it. It may be seen that under the *Aya* system, a priest, a farmer or a member of any group down to the Holeya (untouch-able) could become a *Yajaman*, but only in relation to specific contexts. We came across an old Cheluvadi who proudly declared that he had grown old in the service of the village, and he talked like a *Yajaman*. We also know of one of the biggest farmers who has given, received and repaid nothing, and who is not accorded the honour of being called a *Yajaman*. The *Yajaman* is one who is like a sun around whom his admirers revolve like satellites, and who is widely re-spected and honoured for his capacity to give, receive and repay gifts. He is thought to be the beloved of the gods and the dead.

The word *Yajaman*, a familiar term in Indian sociology, seems to have been used for the first time in the literature by Crooke in 1896. Since then it has acquired wide currency, but it has been used in a manner different from the way in which we propose to use it here. From Crooke to Wiser it has been used to indicate one who could hire a Brahman, or a Brahman's clientèle, or as a term pertaining to the relations between the landed and the landless. These earlier studies rightly noted that *Dharma* is a universal term applicable to the total context of the village society, but they failed to realise that the term *Yajaman* is an equally all-embracing concept. Both are flexible concepts and both are changing concepts, ever ready to acquire extensions of meaning.

In short, we propose that the *Yajaman* should be looked at in a total context, which was not done in earlier studies of the subject. The institution of *Yajaman* is not confined to societies, tribal or non-tribal societies, and *Malenad* or non-*Malenad* villages. It may be found in Hindu as well as Muslim villages. We propose to argue that the position of the *Yajaman* can be understood only in its total context.

The *Aya* system is an archaic system. Together with other village institutions it forms a total complex in its own right. Its various functions may be listed as economic, religious, moral, political, legal, aesthetic and morphological. These functions affect human relations at various levels—involving individuals, groups and villages.

Economic Function: The production and distribution system in Shivapur rests on the foundation of exchanges of goods and services. In this economy land wealth has an important role, but its main focus is not a market economy. Production is not, except on a small scale in very recent years, meant for export. What is produced is largely ploughed back, through the local social system, for internal consumption. However, a market economy does exist to a small extent. Thus one notes that Shivapur operates a dual economy. As in a modern economy, there is specialisation of services, involving corporate life. But this should not be likened to trade union bargaining. For one thing, the Shivapur occupational groups do not possess any formal mechanisms for bargaining, and such unity of action as may be seen is a temporary phenomenon called forth by crises. For another, the trade union operates on an impersonal basis, whereas the *Ayagaras* are linked on a more personal basis.

The economy moves on the wheels of such principles as give-and-take and reciprocity. Though competition and bargaining exist, they are very infrequent, and in any case not at all formalised. They occur as momentary events, indeed as deviants from the norm, and are soon consigned to oblivion. Thus one sees a high degree of personalisation and humanisation in all areas of the economy.

The specific characteristics of the *Aya* economy may be briefly summarised. Whatever is produced or sold, the process and transaction involved are not merely those of purchase and sale, for they involve, as a rule, extra-economic elements like morality and religion. A man who expects more in return should give more and repay more. If he fails to do so, he loses his status and standing in the community. But when a man receives, there are no formal specific conditions, though there are implied expectations. If, however, such conditions are explicitly verbalised, then such conditions are confined to the purely economic aspects of a transaction.

The *Aya*, the unmeasured and unconditional gift, is regarded as the highest gift. Though the quantum may not be overtly specified, the gift is lodged in a specific context of time, place and circumstances. All along the social hierarchical system there are perpetual series of transactions of giving, receiving and repaying. All who are economically better off, ritualistically higher or gifted with greater skill, participate in a competition to maintain their positions by attempting to give more through the system of gift exchanges. Such a competition and struggle sets in motion a series of rights and obligations regarding services rendered and services received.

The motif of sharing one's possessions with others dominates the economy. It is this which is the moving principle underlying the gift exchanges involving giving, receiving and repaying. It is this eventually that determines one's position and status in a group, in a caste and in the village as a whole. The *Aya* is, under the economy, inherited as a matter of customary right. The pattern of giving, receiving and repaying has become so much ingrained into the consciousness of the social order that the receiver does not feel inferior nor the giver superior. This is evident from the fact that the receiver claims a proprietary right over the gifts he receives. The right is not merely material, but also spiritual, since it involves the sanction of *Dharma*. Honour and generosity, which are noticeable during a wedding or the building of a house, reveal the element of conspicuous consumption in the economy. The economic life of Shivaput, it must be noted, is related to other aspects.

Religion and Morals: The different functionaries of Shivapur may look either like men operating the economy or like men without economic roles. But this is misleading and happens only when one looks at the situation from a modern point of view. It would be equally fallacious to dichotomise them sharply into religious and non-religious functions. From the point of view of the gift exchange system, the role of the priest is ambiguous. On the one hand, he gets paid for his services, and, on the other, his services are not reducible to modern economic ones. The priest and his associates are given gifts and food during the ceremony of 'welcoming the dead'. The temple and the gods are given gifts. The priest, as a mediator for natural benefits such as rain, is important. People also seek his mediatory services when they desire wealth and children. Though the priest may invoke the favours of supernatural powers, the benefits aimed at are material.

Recently the goddess Dyamavva was offered a rain-propitiation ceremony and her ceremonial chariot was drawn in the village. When rains still fail, the people fall back on the idea of *Karma* to explain it and console themselves. The rain-propitiation ceremonies are performed during the sowing time. The harvest feasts and festivals are also occasions on which the priests are called upon to propitiate the gods and the venerable dead. During the harvest festival, they scatter cooked food to the winds as a gift with the expectation of greater repayment.

Children are also regarded as emissaries of the gods. During the *Jokumara* festival, children donning masques go about asking for gifts, and they must be given. During the *Holi* festival they get gifts, and also during the *Moharrum* festival. On all these occasions it is forbidden to refuse gifts to children. Offering of such gifts is regarded as a great source of earning merit (*punya*). The system of gifts to children is a complex with a unity of its own. Thus one notes that the ethical order of *Dharma* raises the level of the economy to an ethical position, and ensures that the needy, the poor, the untouchable, and all the like are benefitted.

Politics: The political life of the village also revolves round the ideal of *Dharma*, which underlies the whole of the gift society. The *Aya* has created politically an aristocracy since it involves hierarchy. The principle of *noblesse oblige* characterises all groups, not merely the top ones as some writers on Indian village society have claimed. The priest is expected to attend all groups equally.

One who gives in a modest and disinterested manner is highly valued. This kind of attitude underlies the behaviour of farmers who, when they give less, feel apologetic about it and always say, 'Next time I shall give more'. The *Yajamans*, whether of the street, caste or village, get leadership and headship automatically. The *Yajamans*, of course, are those who practise the principle of *noblesse oblige*. Thus the *Aya* confers rank, status and political leadership on the participants in the system.

Law: The traditional *Aya* system recognises rights of individuals and groups and of the community. There are individual rights to inherit the *Aya*, proprietary rights, rights to service and rights to extra gifts for extra service. The collective rights become manifest during house-building, weddings and the harvest. There are group rights involved in temple and village property. The sanctions behind these rights are both formal and informal. They are negative as well as positive. A man who conforms to the traditional system of rights is respected, and invested with *Maryade* (prestige). He is referred to as a *Dharmistha* or one who follows the path of *Dharma*. He is also the *Yajaman*. He who does not conform is ridiculed and even boycotted. This customary legal order coexists with the modern law of the courts in the urban areas, although having a greater hold than the modern, positive law. The sanction of customary law is, ultimately, the rod of *Dharma*.

Aesthetics: Ornaments have a social aspect insofar as they indicate social position. They have a kinship aspect, since they are referred to as given by kinsman or kinswoman so-and-so in a certain context. They have a ritual aspect, since they are connected with religious rites and ceremonies. And they also have an economic aspect, since they function as security in times of financial crisis.

A village woman loaded with ornaments may be scorned as gaudy by her city-bred sister, but the villagers consider the decline of ornaments a decline in aesthetic sense. The ornaments given during puberty rites, weddings, death ceremonies, etc., are all part of a system of gift exchanges. The bride herself is given away in marriage as a gift and she repays it by bringing a good name to her parents. The gifts given during puberty rites are regarded as being repaid when a girl delivers her first child.

Other aesthetic occasions in Shivapur are concerned with folk-songs, the *Jokumara* festival and the tiger masque during the *Moharrum*. The use of the ancient Hindu epics of Ramayana and Mahabharata in the rustic open-air drama (*Bailata*) may be mentioned in this connection. There are also the ballads and the devotional songs (*Keertana*). The decorations of the images of the deities also involve a display of aesthetic sense. The dance, too, is part of life, and it breaks into a joyous tumult during the *Holi* and *Moharrum* festivals. During the *Nagarapanchime* (snake festival), songs and music are indulged in. During the harvest time there is dance and music. Open-air dramas are staged soon after the harvest is over. The farmers who have harvested give back to the community by having them staged. Even the stage is ceremonially worshipped before the show opens. Lastly, the innumerable fairs and festivals of the village give scope for colour, movement and rhythm.

Morphology: As we have seen, both the ritual calendar and the secular calendar exist, but each with a specialised function. Gifts flow all the year round during different seasons and at different places. They have to be given when a daughter is sent away from the natal home for the first time. They are given, too, when she comes home from her husband's place for the first time. Later on she gets gifts at all religious festivals, starting with the *Nagarapanchime*. During the *Nagarapanchime*, a brother is supposed to go and fetch her home and he must then offer her the gift of a saree. It is a highly seasonal gift made at a time when nature is emerald green with joy and promise. There is thus a link between human and natural seasons. During the *Deepavali* (festival of lights), she is again brought home and given gifts. This coincides with the harvest time, and a basketful of new grain is heaped at her feet. In all these matters, the ritual calendar is reckoned in terms of the moon's position. However, modern calendars and watches are used in secular contexts.

November brings a lull in the work and it is the month when the farmers are comparatively free. The village fairs and festivals invariably come after the harvest, and thus one can see co-ordination between man's and nature's gifts. During the festival of a village deity, the whole extended family gathers to celebrate. They also gather during the harvest celebrations. During the *Shravana* (August), the *Deepavali*, and harvest, it is forbidden for a brother to deny any gift asked for by a sister, and equally a sister cannot refuse a brother's gifts. Priests and other religious dignitaries, beggars, and mendicants, all are given gifts during these occasions. Thus sharing and giving on some pretext or other is the most characteristic feature of the *Aya*.

To realise fully the fundamental meaning of the *Aya* system, one must set it against the background of its multifarious aspects and functions. The *Aya* comes to be seen as a complex pattern of relationships. Only when seen as a totality do these relationships reveal their inner meaning and essence, which lie in the dynamics of giving, receiving and repaying. The forms of payment are many, such as *Kanike, Dakshine, Ulipi, Aya*, etc. Such gifts involve nonmaterial as well as material values. The basic motivational force behind the working of the system is the need of everybody for everybody. This brings human beings into personal relationships in the system. One's position is defined by these factors. The dominant forces are generosity, hospitality, prestige and honour. It is for these that men seem to bend their social action. But the spiritual element in it is the *Dharma*, which links the living to the living, to the dead, and to the gods. It also links man to nature, and tradition is the bedrock upon which the system is based.

2

Many students of Indian village society from Crooke to Beidelman, mostly foreigners, have attempted to characterise it as 1, typically Indian, 2, caste-bound, and 3, agricultural. Such attempts have tried to extract the meaning of the social pattern either in terms of partial derivation from tradition or from a totally modern perspective. They have missed its actual movement and dynamism. The intricate details have escaped their notice.

We have shown that its basis is a gift system involving a

series of exchange transactions developing around the acts of giving, receiving and repaying. Our model is close to the one revealed in Mauss' collection of primitive or traditional archaic societies based on the principle of gift exchange. Thus we argue that the Indian village society is not unique, since it belongs to a world-wide family of social systems, to be found in Africa, Australia, Asia, America and Europe.

The *Potlatch* institution of Samoa in Polynesia, for instance, is characterised by a hierarchy of chiefs and nobles, one competing with the other in hospitality and the giving of gifts in order to establish his rank, honour and privilege. Here, too, the gift involves the obligation to repay. This principle underlies the life of an individual from birth to death. The chiefs and nobles are expected to maintain *Mana* (prestige and honour) by giving gifts. The theory of gifts and their obligatory repayment is the basis of the clan and the tribe. The recipient accepts the gift as of right. The giver and the receiver are bound in a spiritual and moral bond.

The Tlingit and the Haida tribes of Alaska also exemplify the gift society. In this society, respect for one another is shown through gifts as in Shivapur, where one's *Maryade* (prestige) depends on the giving of gifts. These tribes also practice the *potlatch*. At fairs, festivals, and banquets, there are hierarchical gatherings at which economic, religious, social and political transactions take place at different levels of the hierarchy. These are comparable to the caste ranks of Shivapur. Gifts are moral as well as material, since they are obligatory.

The Tsimshian and the Kwakiutl tribes of British Columbia are non-agricultural, fishing/hunting societies. They are a contrast to the Polynesian, Melanesian or North American Indian tribal societies with an agricultural economy. They have well-built houses. They are wonderful carvers and there is a flourishing cedar industry. As in the *Aya* system, here too there are seasonal gifts. In winter, towns and villages observe ceremonies which involve a series of gift exchanges. These are given with no overt obligation for repayment, but repayment is expected and made on a better scale.

Fiji has an institution comparable to the gift system. It is called the *Kerekere* season, when it is forbidden to deny gifts. Children, especially, must not be denied what they ask. This is comparable to the *Jokumara* ceremony of Shivapur.

Among the Trobriand islanders there is the *Kula,* a variant of the *Potlatch* institution. This is a society of pearl-traders. The *Kula* involves inter-tribal and intra-tribal commerce and trade spread over the whole island. Like the *Aya*, this is an aristocratic social order involving the ideal of *noblesse oblige*. The giver and the receiver are united by a bond which is at once material, moral and religious. Its commercial character is noticeable in that property transactions, pledges and borrowings take place within it. This is part of a vast complex of presentations and counter-presentations whose motives are analogous to those of the *Aya*. Gifts have to be made on arrival, departure, on first meetings, etc. There is an exchange of shells on such occasions. The chief motives are obligation, self-interest and magnanimity. Gifts are given during ceremonies. The manner in which gifts are exchanged is comparable to that of the *Potlatch* of the Kwakiutl or that of the *Aya* of Shiva-put. The ritual gifts to gods and spirits are called the *Pokala* and *Kaributu* gifts. These are solicitory gifts made to seek supernatural help for increasing trade and prosperity.

Among the Eskimos, another fishing society, innumerable festivals are celebrated to invoke superior powers for increasing the catch of the fish. These are comparable to the harvest festivals in Shivapur.

Among the Koryak and Chukchee tribes of Northern Siberia, and among their neighbours, the Yurit tribe, there is a *Potlatch*. They have seasonal festivals during winter when thanksgiving is offered to the gods for the good collection. After they have consumed their fill, whatever is left over is thrown to the winds, and this parallels the Shivapur harvest ceremony when food is also given to the winds.

In Russia there is what is known as the *Koleda* custom, according to which children go from house to house begging for flour, which they must not be refused.

In Australia, there is recorded evidence of proprietary rights being vested in the receiver to the gifts he receives. In hunting societies, game collected has to be given to one's father-in-law and mother-in-law or, as in Fiji, to one's maternal uncle. With such gifts go duties and obligations.

Among the Andaman islanders there is well-organised inter-group hospitality involving gifts. These are given during fairs and festivals, and are obligatory and moral. They are considered as signs of friendship, and people vie with one another to give such gifts.

The above examples, like the *Aya* system of Shivapur, reveal societies based on the ideals of generosity, *noblesse oblige,* harmony, honour and economic interdependence. As in the case of the *Aya*, there is never any explicit mention of what is to be given. There is merely an implied expectation in appropriate contexts. Hence to give more is regarded as the ideal. It is feared that if one gives less, it will harm one. Mention may be made here of the idea of *kula* involving the *kudu*. If the giver gives less, the *kula* (gift) will bite the giver with its teeth, the *kudu*! The repayment must be made with interest if it is not given at the right time. If one does not give with interest at that time, the *kudu* will bite one right through to the bones. Under the *Aya* system, one who gets less on two successive occasions may desert the *Ayadakula*.

The point of our comparisons is not that the *Aya* system and the compared examples are identical. Rather it is that the same basic principles operate in different contexts while still retaining the same fundamental character.

3

In the concluding section we shall attempt to show the material and spiritual mechanism of the gift. It is economic, moral and spiritual. Each of these aspects is distinct and yet is connected with the others. Ultimately it has spiritual foundations. In the *Aya* system, the concept of *Dharma* constitutes this spiritual foundation. Mauss refers to modern societies in Scandinavia, where contracts are fulfilled through exchanges of gifts; in France, where there is keen competition to offer ceremonial gifts; and in Germany, where an invitation is binding and has to be returned (*Revanchieren*). Under the *Aya*, the sanctions of the system are material or non-material, and so they are in the above examples from modern Europe.

The relations between economy and morality, economy and law, and economy and religion, in the simpler forms of the gift society, have been misunderstood as exemplifications of the barter or 'natural' economy. Of course, nothing could be farther from the truth. It is arguable that even the modern credit system is based on the gift idea. What was missed is the many-sided complexity of the gift in the older system. It is true that there is an element of barter, but there are also other elements which, so to say, draw it into a total social context. The functions of the modern system of wages and so on are here performed by the gifts. Thus justice itself is regarded as a self-adjusting mechanism of the gift system.

We have in the gift a compound of moral, economic and socio-political aspects. The utilitarian, religious, ethical, social, political and economic functions are combined into an interdependent totality which ensures harmony for all. The gift system is also the result of the limitations of environment that are inevitable in a closed system. In such a system, friendship and harmony become imperative. No doubt tensions and conflicts do arise, but they are quickly solved or just soft-pedalled till they become socially harmless. Land and wealth are regarded as means towards one's own and one's fellow men's happiness, but are not considered as ends in themselves. The motto is that happiness lies in sharing everything.

Evaluation

It is our contention here that though students of the *Aya* system have so far studied it thoroughly, they have done so only from a limited perspective. They have subjected one of its many aspects to thorough study, leaving out the rest. For instance, we have excellent studies of its economic aspect. There is nothing wrong in such a method, provided it is clearly understood that a true understanding arises only from a study of the totality of a system. But unfortunately many writers have invariably mistaken one aspect of the *Aya* for the total phenomenon.

Idealised, the *Aya* system appears to be one of peace and contentment, where people help the needy and where benevolence is the pervading spirit. It is also seen ideally as self-sufficient. Its strength has been attributed to the *noblesse oblige* of the higher castes, the Brahman in particular. Power has been identified with the high castes. But our study of Shivapur must dispel these illusions. Actually we found the village not at all self-sufficient. We found in its social system scope for conflict and tension, though also a tendency to reduce them. We found the idea of a single dominant caste untenable, since we discovered a pattern of inter-action between castes, which tended to maintain a kind of balance of power. We found the power relations based on a wider dispersion. We saw that the *noblesse oblige* attitude was not the monopoly of any single caste, but spread over the whole hierarchy.

It has been contended that the *Aya* is based on the principle of ritual pollution. The twice-born is the landowner. He observes rituals of pollution and purity, and in this lies his superior social status. The once-born is landless, is less ritualistically inclined and hence inferior. This again is a picture which scarcely corresponds to things as we saw them in Shivapur. We found that the basis of the *Aya* was essentially economic, though associated with other non-material factors. We found the landed-landless dichotomy to be not necessarily one of the superior-inferior or exploiter-exploited type. We found all groups inclined towards ritualistic behaviour. In short, we would seriously question the identification of land with power.

There are some students of the Indian village society who have regarded it as an exclusively economic system. They have seen the social dynamics of the village in terms of a conflict between the higher and lower castes, and this has been further cast in the form of an economic conflict between the landed and the landless. This is again a power relation approach, though power is conceived of in exclusively economic terms. The landed alone are regarded as the *Yajamans* in this view. Our study has clearly shown that the landed-landless conflict is by no means the key economic factor of the *Aya* system. The idea that the landed alone were *Yajamans,* we found, was not true.

In Shivapur we came across the case of the landowner who was not regarded as a *Yajaman* and the case of a Cheluvadi untouchable who was considered as a *Yajaman.* The allied view that the dominant caste, on the one hand, and the occupational groups on trade union lines, on the other, maintain the social system, has been found to be untrue. We have found that when a caste tends to be too strong there are counter-forces which operate to maintain a power balance. The occupational groups are not based on the individualism of the modern trade union, since they are not as formal and impersonal.

There is a theory that the village society may be seen as a reflection, or rather imitation, of the kingly style of life. In the kingly style, the Kshatriya is dominant. But in Shivapur we found no functional Kshatriya group at all. This theory assumes that the higher castes tend to model themselves on the kingly style. This assumption is not borne out by our study. Imitation may actually be in both directions.

We may also dismiss as inadequate the view that the village society is based on simple economic exchange or barter. Our whole study has established beyond dispute the complexity of the exchange system.

The argument that the survival of the village society must

be attributed to the fact of its isolation from the outside market also breaks down once it is realised that the village society is neither fully self-sufficient nor closed. In Shivapur we saw how there existed clearly noticeable inter-village relations. The Shivapur artisans enjoyed considerable spatial mobility.

Some have held that in the *Malenad* areas cash crops are grown and hence there is a cash economy, and this does not permit the rise of the *Aya* (or the *Yajaman*) system. Similarly the *Aya* system is supposed to be possible only among Hindu villages, on the assumption that Muslim Bengal had no *Aya* system. In Shivapur we have seen that both the cash economy and the traditional economy can coexist. We have also found there Muslims functioning as part of the traditional system.

There is a school of thought which believes that the observance of ritual rules by the higher castes and the absorption of pollution by the lower castes leads to social integration. In Shivapur, however, we have found that not all higher caste men have washermen and that the untouchables have given up leather-work, and yet there is no social decomposition.

The factionalism theory may also be disposed of briefly. In this theory, the village society is supposed to be sustained by its factionalism. This view assumes that it gives bargaining power to groups which get things by threatening factional conflict. The fact that the supply of labour exceeds demand is believed to have given the lower castes their bargaining power. Because of this they are supposed to shift their allegiance. But, actually, in Shivapur, we found such shifting of allegiance very rare. We found inapplicable to Shivapur the model of a vertical opposition of dominant castes and lower castes, undermining the inter-caste unity.

The feudal interpretation of the *Aya* is also unacceptable. The nature of the feudal relations and the exclusive monopoly of land power associated with it have no relevance here. Of course, similarities such as hierarchy and land-ownership should not blind us to fundamental differences.

We are now in a position to state that all the above efforts to see the village society in modern terms are too simple and limited to be true. They have failed to consider the totality of human behaviour under specific circumstances and have failed to see that such behaviour can be accounted for only by the multiple factors which help shape social structure and dynamics. These factors which determine total social configurations may be established and measured with a reasonable degree of precision. They point to the important truth that social existence, indeed all life, is an act which involves the difficulty of co-ordinating the multiple determinants of life. Our study of Shivapur has shown that our village life has proved itself equal to such a task.

GLOSSARY

Adharma; that which is opposed to *Dharma*. See *Dharma*
Agasa; Washerman
Agasi Bagilu; Village entrance gate
Allah; God (according to Islam)
Alategalu or **Alegalu;** Measured grain
Arati; Vessel-like lamp
Artha; Wealth, material welfare
Aya; Exchange of goods and services based on the principles of gift
Ayagara; recipient of *Aya*
Ayadakula; family giving *Aya*

Bab; a kind of ritual gift to priests and temples
Badiga; carpenter
Bandegalu; grain from the harvest-cart
Basava; leader of Lingayats who lived in twelfth century A.D. Also means bull
Basava Jayanti; birthday celebration of Basava
Basinga; wedding crown of flowers
Bhajan; religious song or hymn
Bhajanamandal; prayer meeting
Bhat; Brahman priest
Bhiksha; gift to priests, mendicants, etc.
Bile; white
Birappa; god of shepherds

Chakkadi; bullock-cart
Cheluvadi; untouchable

Dakshine; a gift to priests made in multiples of five
Deepavali; festival of lights
Desai; landlord
Dharma; a comprehensive term denoting duty, religion, morality, law, etc., all combined in one

Dharmistha; ideal observer of Dharma
Dindi; Maratha festival
Duragavva; goddess of the Cheluvadis
Dwija; twice-born
Dyamavva; goddess of fertility

Ganapati; elephant-tusked god of the Hindus
Ganiga; oil-grinder
Godana; gift of cow
Grama; village
Grama Panchayati; village council of elders
Guggala; wedding rite among Lingayats

Habbadaklu; grain of the festival
Hadadi; custom of spreading white cloth during a ritual procession
Hadapad; barber
Hage; grain storing pit
Hiriya; elder
Holeaya; gift of grain to untouchable
Holeya; untouchable
Holi; a festival of the god of love
Hugar; florist

Jaggery; coarse dark brown sugar
Jangam; Lingayat priest
Jati; caste
Jatipanchayat; caste council
Jita; contract labour
Jitagara; contract labourer

Kaigada; loan
Kaiguna; skilful hand
Kama; god of love or physical love
Kambali; blanket
Kanike; a kind of ritual gift
Karahunnime; a festival of bullocks
Kare; black
Kareganiga; black oil grinder
Karejadar; black weaver

Glossary

Karevva; goddess of the Cheluvadis
Karma; the idea that one's actions determine one's destiny
Kayaka; spiritual value of labour
Khandoba; Maratha deity
Kharif; rainy-season crop
Kshatriya; warrior caste
Kula; plough
Kulakarni; village accountant
Kumbar; potter
Kuruba; shepherd
Kushi; extra gift given to lower castes

Madi; ritual purity
Madiga; untouchable
Malenad; coastal and hilly region
Mantra; sacred verse, hymn
Maryade; prestige
Mayevva; goddess of the Madigas
Moharrum; Muslim festival
Moksha; spiritual salvation
Mulla; Muslim priest

Nagarapanchime; festival of snakes
Nidhi; gift of grain to gods and temples

Oni; street

Panchal; artisan
Panchayat; council of elders
Papa; sin
Parada; veil
Pattar; goldsmith
Pattu; trust, faith
Punya; spiritual merit

Rabi; winter crop
Ramzan; Muslim festival

Saree; dress of Hindu woman
Shilpi; stone sculptor

Glossary

Shiva Jayanti; birthday celebration of Shivaji, leader of Marathas
Susaya; overflowing gift of grain

Talawar; village traditional servant
Taluka; subdivision of a district
Teneganike; gift of top grain
Tonga; horse-drawn cab
Tundaya; broken gift of grain

Udi; fold of a saree
Udiakki; ritual rice in the fold of a saree
Ugadi; Hindu New Year Day
Ulipi; a kind of ritual gift
Upajati; sub-caste
Uru; village

Vanki; armlet
Varna; (lit: colour) classical division of Hindu society in ancient India
Vata; hired grain
Vatti; mortgage transaction
Vibhutivile; rite on the occasion of an impending death of a Lingayat

Yajaman; master, owner, elderly person
Yedi; gift of food to gods

APPENDIX

1 *Lingayat*:
  Hiremath
  Chikkamath
  Ganachari
  Mathapati
  Hugar
  Pujar
  Banajiga: (*a*) Adi Banajiga
         (*b*) Sheelavant Banajiga
  Panchamasali
  Panchamasali Totiga
  Sadar
  Jadar: (*a*) Bile Jadar
      (*b*) Kare Jadar
  Ganiga: (*a*) Bile Ganiga
       (*b*) Kare Ganiga
  Hadapad
2 *Brahman*:
  Vaishnava
  Smartha
3 *Jain*:
  Digambara
  Svetambara
4 *Vaishya*
5 *Panchal*:
  Pattar (goldsmith): (*a*) Madi
             (*b*) Sada
             (*c*) local
             (*d*) immigrant
  Badiga (carpenter)
  Kambara (blacksmith)
6 *Maratha*:
  Buruqi
  Jande Rawut
  Kulavadi
  Nadukattu
7 *Rajaput*:
  Singh
  Kayastha
8 *Kuruba*:
  Hattikankana
  Unnikankana
9 *Muslim*:
  Sheikh

Sayada
Moghal
Pathan
10 *Barikar*
11 *Talawar*
12 *Korava*
13 *Holeya*: (*a*) Cheluvadi
        (*b*) Madiga: local
               immigrant

[B] VILLAGE PANTHEON

Male	*Female*
Allah	Banashankari
Basava	Duragavva
Birappa	Dyamavva
Gandhi	Ganga
Ganapati	Gouri
Hanumant	Kalavva
Ishwar	Karevva
Jina	Mayevva
Khandoba	Yellamma
Krishna	
Pitris	
Priest	
Rama	
Ramalinga	
Shivaji	
Vishnu	

Other objects of worship

Agricultural implements (excepting leather goods)

Bilva tree	Cow dung
Books	Monkey
Bull	River, tank, well
Cow	Snake

[C] SOME IMPORTANT FESTIVALS

Basava Jayanti	Karahunnime
Birappana Habba	Krishna Janmastami
Deepavali	Mayevva
Dindi	Moharrum
Gandhi Jayanti	Nagarapanchime
Ganapati	Ramazan
Gouri Habba	Shigi Hunnime
Hirera Habba	Shiva Jayanti
Holi	

BIBLIOGRAPHY

For further reading

[A] BOOKS

Baden-Powell, B. H., *The Land Systems of British India*, 3 Volumes, London, 1892.
Baden-Powell, G. H., *The Indian Village Community*, London, 1896.
Beidelman, Thomas O., *A Comparative Analysis of the Jajamani System*, New York, 1959.
Briggs, G. W., *The Chamars*, Calcutta, 1920.
Campbell, J., *Census of India*, Vol. 1, Calcutta, 1901.
Cox, O. C., *Caste, Class and Race*, New York, 1948.
Crooke, W., *The Tribes and Castes of North Western Provinces and Oudh*, 4 Volumes, Calcutta, 1896.
Crooke, W., *The North-Western Provinces of India*, London, 1897.
Crooke, W., *Natives of Northern India*, London, 1907.
Darling, M. L., *The Punjab Peasant in Prosperity and Debt*, London, 1925.
Darling, M. L., *Wisdom and Waste in the Punjab Village*, London, 1934.
Desai, M. B., *The Rural Economy of Gujarat*, Bombay, 1948.
Dhillon, S. H. S., *Leadership and Groups in a South Indian Village*, New Delhi, 1955.
Dube, S. C., *Indian Village*, London, 1955.
Dubois, J. A., *Hindu Manners, Customs and Ceremonies*, London, 1906.
Enthoven, R. E., *The Ethnographical Survey of Bombay*, Bombay, 1909.
Firth, Raymond, *Economics of the New Zealand Maori*, New Zealand, 1959.
Fuchs, S., *The Children of Hari*, New York, 1951.
Gadgil, D. R., and Gadgil, V. R., *A Survey of Farm Business in Wai Taluka*, Poona, 1940.
Ghurye, G. S., *Caste and Race in India*, London, 1932.
Grant, C., *Gazetter of the Central Provinces*, Bombay, 1870.
Grierson, G. A., *Bihar Peasant Life*, Calcutta, 1885.
Herskovits, M. J., *Economic Anthropology*, New York, 1952.
Hivale, S., *The Pardhans of the Upper Narmada Valley*, Bombay, 1946.
Hocart, A. M., *Caste*, London, 1950.
Ibbetson, D. C. J. and Macglan, E., and Rose, H. A., *A Glossary of the Tribes and Castes of the Punjab and North West Frontier Provinces*, 3 Volumes, 1914.
Jack, J. C., *The Economic Life of a Bengal Village*, Oxford, 1916.
Jayaraman, K. A., *A Study of the Panchayats in Madras*, Bombay, 1947.
Malinowski, Bronislaw, *Argonauts of the Western Pacific*, London, 1922.
Manu, H. H., and Kanitkar, N. V., *Land and Labour in a Deccan Village*, Bombay, 1921.
Marriott, McKim (Ed), *Village India*, Chicago, 1955.
Mauss, Marcel, *The Gift*, London, 1954.
Mayer, A. C., *Land and Society in Malabar*, London, 1952.

161

Bibliography

Nehru, S., *Caste and Credit in the Rural Area*, New York, 1932.
Polanyi, K., Arensberg, C. M. and Pearson, H., *Trade and Market in the Early Empires*, New York, 1957.
Radcliffe-Brown, A. R., *The Andaman Islanders*, Cambridge, 1922.
Shukla, J. B., *Life and Labour in a Gujarat Taluka*, Calcutta, 1937.
Singh, T., *Poverty and Social Change*, London, 1945.
Singh, M., *The Depressed Classes*, Bombay, 1947.
Slater, G., *Some South Indian Villages*, Madras, 1918.
Tax, Sol, *Penny Capitalism*, Washington, 1953.
Thurston, E., *Ethnographic in Southern India*, Madras, 1909.
Wiser, W. H., *The Hindu Jajamani System*, Lucknow, 1936.

[B] PAPERS

Altekar, M. D., 'Caste System and its Relation to Social and Economic Life', *The Annals of the American Academy of Political and Social Science*, Vol. 233, 1944, pp. 183-187.
Ames, Michael M., 'Ritual Prestations and the Structure of the Sinhalese Pantheon', *Yale University South East Series*, 1966.
Beals, A. R., 'Interplay among Factors of Change in a Mysore Village,' *Village India*, Chicago, 1955.
Cohn, B. S., 'The Changing Status of a Depressed Caste,' *Village India*, Chicago, 1955.
Cooke, W., 'Chamars,' *Census of India*, London, 1901, Vol. I, pp. 169-175.
Eames, E., 'Population and Economic Structure of an Indian Rural Community,' *Eastern Anthropologist*, Lucknow, Vol. 8, Nos. 3 and 4, pp. 173-181.
Gough, E. K., 'The Social Structure of a Tanjore Village,' *The Economic Weekly*, Bombay, Vol. IV, No. 21, pp. 531-536.
Gould, Harold A., 'The Hindu Jajamani System,' *Southwestern Journal of Anthropology*, Albuquerque, Vol. 15, No. 3, pp. 227-234.
Harper, Edward, 'Two Systems of Economic Exchange in Village India,' *American Anthropologist*, California, Vo. 61, No. 5, Part 1, pp. 760-778.
Lewis, Oscar, 'Caste and the Jajamani System,' *Village Life in Northern India*, Urbana, 1958, pp. 55-87.
Majumdar, D. N., Pradhan, M. C., Sen, C., and Misra, S., 'Intercaste Relations in Cohanakallan, a Village near Lucknow,' *Eastern Anthropologist*, Lucknow, Vol. 8, Nos. 3 and 4, pp. 191-214.
Marriott, McKim, 'Little Communities in an Indigenous Civilization, *Village India*, Chicago, 1955, pp. 171-222.
Mandelbaum, D. G., 'The World and the World View of the Kota,' *Village India*, Chicago, 1955, pp. 223-255.
Mayer, A. C., 'Some Hierarchical Aspects of Caste,' *South Western Journal of Anthropology*, Albuquerque, Vol. 12, No. 2, pp. 117-144.
Miller, E. J., 'Village Structure in North Kerala,' *Economic Weekly*, Bombay, Vol. 4, No. 6, pp. 159-164.

Bibliography

Misra, S., 'Earnings of Village Servants in U. P.,' *The Eastern Anthropologist*, Lucknow, Vol. 5, Nos. 2 and 3, pp. 96-100.

Newell, William H., 'The Brahman and Caste Isogamy in North India,' *Journal of the Royal Anthropological Institute*, London.

Opler, Morris E., and Singh, R. D., 'The Division of Labour in an Indian Village,' *A Reader in General Anthropology*, New York, 1948.

Patnaik, N., 'A Survey of the Economic and Social Conditions of the Chamars of Barpali in Orissa,' *The Economic Weekly*, Bombay, Vol. 5, No. 37, pp. 103-105; No. 38, pp. 1034-1036; No. 39, pp. pp. 1065-1066.

Pocock, David, 'Notes on Jajamani Relationships,' *Contributions to Indian Sociology*, The Hague, pp. 78-95.

Reddy, N. S., 'Functional Relationship of Lohars in a Northern Indian Village,' *The Eastern Anthropologist*, Lucknow, Vol. 8, Nos. 3 and 4, pp. 129-140

Shah, A. M., 'A Dispersed Hamlet in the Panchmals,' *The Economic Weekly*, Annual Number, Bombay, pp. 109-116.

Smith, M. W., 'Social Structure in the Punjab,' *The Economic Weekly*, Bombay, Vol. 5, No. 47, pp. 1293-1298.

Srinivas, M. N., 'The Social System of a Mysore Village,' *Village India*, Chicago, 1955, pp. 1-36.

Trent, S., 'Irrigation and Socio-Economic Change in a Mysore Village,' *The Economic Weekly*, Bombay, Vol. 7, No. 37, pp. 1091-1094.

Weber, Max, 'India: The Brahman and the Castes,' *Max Weber: Essays in Sociology*, Oxford, 1946.

[C] JOURNALS

It is worth mentioning that much important work on the subject is also available in Journals, such as *Africa, The American Anthropologist*, the *Journal of Asian Studies*, the *Journal of Asian and African Studies*, *Contributions to Indian Sociology*, Eastern Anthropologist, Ethnology, Royal Anthropological Institute, Human Organisation (*See its special number on Jajamani system*), *International Journal of Comparative Sociology*, *Man in India, The South Western Journal of Anthropology*. Some of the references already mentioned above include papers published in these various Journals.

INDEX

Index

Index

Index

Payment, 10, 74, 81
Pilgrimage, 6
Planning commission, 2
Pokala, 148
Politics, 13, 14, 124; and
    administration, 119–21; political
    awareness, 121; consciousness, 13;
    decision, 14; leadership, 121, 143
Polynesia, 147
Population, 8, 92, 116; pressure, 91;
    problems, 98
Potlach, 147, 148
Prestations, 72, 75, 77
Prestige, 29, 38, 77, 82
Property, 96, 98, 135, 144
Puberty rites, 30, 66
Puja, 19
Punishment, 15
Punya, 24, 94, 138, 143
Punyakatha, 57
Purana, 57
Purity and pollution, 16, 19, 25, 26,
    30, 32, 33, 38, 39, 66, 71, 74, 113,
    115, 122, 151

Rabi, 9, 81
Ramayana, 69
Ramazan, 12, 59
Relationships, artisan-nonartisan, 52;
    competitive, 97; economic, 35, 37,
    53; equal-inequal, 48; horizontal
    and vertical, 48
Religious group, 6, 12; dignitaries, 10,
    46, 52, 59, 83; functionaries, 54, 59,
    60
Revanchieren, 150
Rights and responsibilities, 50–74
Rites of passage, 12
Rituals, 50, 51, 56, 60, 94; ritual bath,
    57, 60, 94, 122
Rotti, 66
Rupee, 54, 88, 91, 107, 117

Sacrament, 56
Sacred, 79
Sada, 60, 61
Samoa, 147
Sanction, 24, 53, 75, 77, 84, 93, 111,
    142, 144
Sant, 56, 59
Scarcity, 91, 98
Secular, 79, 127, 145
Security, 10, 90–3, 118, 130, 135
Self-sufficiency, 46, 50, 75, 151, 153
Shehanai, 129
Shilpi, 21
Shivaji, 21, 122; Shivajayanti, 13, 59
Shravana, 146

Sin, 58, 71, 75
Social structure, 17–37
Social, 26, 53, 80, 90, 96, 111, 151;
    context, 1; configuration, 154;
    decomposition, 153; dynamics, 24,
    154; existence, 48, 50, 59, 73, 93,
    154; forces, 73; foundation, 73;
    fabric, 47, 48, 50, 90; function, 39;
    harmony, 107; integration, 153; life,
    47, 72, 96; map, 35; matrix, 71;
    mechanism, 47; model, 24; order,
    91, 92, 96, 108, 113; prescription,
    72; problems, 2; pulse, 111;
    relations, 1, 74, 83, 93, 108, 109,
    125; scale, 55, 89; system, 11, 15,
    17, 40, 41, 43, 48, 49, 52, 90, 91, 95,
    127, 140, 151, 152
Status, 17–22, 27, 33, 44, 46, 49, 50, 55,
    56, 58, 60, 61, 65, 68, 72, 73, 78, 79,
    80, 105, 130, 131, 151; economic,
    44, 61, 63, 80, 92, 96; ritual, 19, 42,
    44, 57, 63–5
Strength and values, 74–95
Sudra, 16
Susaya, 55

Tali, 61
Talisman, 60–2
Temporal, 91, 94
Tonga, 5
Trade union, 40, 109, 152
Trade unionism, 78, 109, 152
Traditional: foundation 1, 113;
    payment, 10; service, 128; system,
    101, 121, 125–7, 129, 137, 138, 144
Transaction, 53, 72, 82, 100, 116, 117
Tundaya, 55
Tundugalu, 83

Udi, 63, 126
Udiakki, 20, 66
Ugadi, 58, 69
Ulipi, 42, 43, 49, 54, 57, 59, 62, 83,
    126, 146
Unnikankan, 22
Universal suffrage, 133
Uppar, 52
Upa-Jati, 16
Uru, 14
Usage, 15

Values, 3, 5, 7, 12, 15, 17, 24, 27, 40,
    57, 58, 60, 74, 78, 79, 93, 94, 99,
    100, 102, 108, 110, 111, 115, 121,
    121, 133, 137, 146
Vanki, 61
Varna, 16, 17, 21

Index

The International Library of
Sociology
and Social Reconstruction

Edited by W. J. H. SPROTT
Founded by KARL MANNHEIM

ROUTLEDGE & KEGAN PAUL
BROADWAY HOUSE, CARTER LANE, LONDON, E.C.4

CONTENTS

PRINTED IN GREAT BRITAIN BY HEADLEY BROTHERS LTD
109 KINGSWAY LONDON WC2 AND ASHFORD KENT

GENERAL SOCIOLOGY

Brown, Robert. Explanation in Social Science. *208 pp. 1963. (2nd Impression 1964.) 25s.*

Gibson, Quentin. The Logic of Social Enquiry. *240 pp. 1960. (2nd Impression 1963.) 24s.*

Goldschmidt, Professor Walter. Understanding Human Society. *272 pp. 1959. 21s.*

Homans, George C. Sentiments and Activities: Essays in Social Science. *336 pp. 1962. 32s.*

Jarvie, I. C. The Revolution in Anthropology. *Foreword by Ernest Gellner. 272 pp. 1964. 40s.*

Johnson, Harry M. Sociology: a Systematic Introduction. *Foreword by Robert K. Merton. 710 pp. 1961. (4th Impression 1964.) 42s.*

Mannheim, Karl. Essays on Sociology and Social Psychology. *Edited by Paul Keckskemeti. With Editorial Note by Adolph Lowe. 344 pp. 1953. 30s.*

Systematic Sociology: An Introduction to the Study of Society. *Edited by J. S. Erös and Professor W. A. C. Stewart. 220 pp. 1957. (2nd Impression 1959.) 24s.*

Martindale, Don. The Nature and Types of Sociological Theory. *292 pp. 1961. (2nd Impression 1965.) 35s.*

Maus, Heinz. A Short History of Sociology. *234 pp. 1962. (2nd Impression 1965.) 28s.*

Myrdal, Gunnar. Value in Social Theory: A Collection of Essays on Methodology. *Edited by Paul Streeten. 332 pp. 1958. (2nd Impression 1962.) 32s.*

Ogburn, William F., and Nimkoff, Meyer F. A Handbook of Sociology. *Preface by Karl Mannheim. 656 pp. 46 figures. 38 tables. 5th edition (revised) 1964. 40s.*

Parsons, Talcott, and Smelser, Neil J. Economy and Society: A Study in the Integration of Economic and Social Theory. *362 pp. 1956. (3rd Impression 1964.) 35s.*

Rex, John. Key Problems of Sociological Theory. *220 pp. 1961. (3rd Impression 1965.) 25s.*

Stark, Werner. The Fundamental Forms of Social Thought. *280 pp. 1962. 32s.*

FOREIGN CLASSICS OF SOCIOLOGY

Durkheim, Emile. Suicide. A Study in Sociology. *Edited and with an Introduction by George Simpson. 404 pp. 1952. (2nd Impression 1963.) 30s.*

Socialism and Saint-Simon. *Edited with an Introduction by Alvin W. Gouldner. Translated by Charlotte Sattler from the edition originally edited with an Introduction by Marcel Mauss. 286 pp. 1959. 28s.*

Professional Ethics and Civic Morals. *Translated by Cornelia Brookfield. 288 pp. 1957. 30s.*

Gerth, H. H., and Mills, C. Wright. From Max Weber: Essays in Sociology. *502 pp. 1948. (5th Impression 1964.) 35s.*

Tönnies, Ferdinand. Community and Association. *(Gemeinschaft und Gesellschaft.) Translated and Supplemented by Charles P. Loomis. Foreword by Pitirim A. Sorokin. 334 pp. 1955. 28s.*

SOCIAL STRUCTURE

Andrzejewski, Stanislaw. Military Organization and Society. *With a Foreword by Professor A. R. Radcliffe-Brown. 226 pp. 1 folder. 1954. 21s.*

Cole, G. D. H. Studies in Class Structure. *220 pp. 1955. (3rd Impression 1964.) 21s.*

Coontz, Sydney H. Population Theories and the Economic Interpretation. *202 pp. 1957. (2nd Impression 1961.) 25s.*

Coser, Lewis. The Functions of Social Conflict. *204 pp. 1956. (2nd Impression 1965.) 18s.*

Glass, D. V. (Ed.). Social Mobility in Britain. *Contributions by J. Berent, T. Bottomore, R. C. Chambers, J. Floud, D. V. Glass, J. R. Hall, H. T. Himmelweit, R. K. Kelsall, F. M. Martin, C. A. Moser, R. Mukherjee, and W. Ziegel. 420 pp. 1954. (2nd Impression 1963.) 40s.*

Kelsall, R. K. Higher Civil Servants in Britain: From 1870 to the Present Day. *268 pp. 31 tables. 1955. 25s.*

Marsh, David C. The Changing Social Structure in England and Wales, 1871-1961. *288 pp. 2nd edition 1965. In preparation.*

Ossowski, Stanislaw. Class Structure in the Social Consciousness. *212 pp. 1963. 25s.*

SOCIOLOGY AND POLITICS

Barbu, Zevedei. Democracy and Dictatorship: Their Psychology and Patterns of Life. *300 pp. 1956. 28s.*

Crick, Bernard. The American Science of Politics: Its Origins and Conditions. *284 pp. 1959. 28s.*

Kornhauser, William. The Politics of Mass Society. *272 pp. 20 tables. 1960. (2nd Impression 1965.) 28s.*

Laidler, Harry W. Social-Economic Movements: An Historical and Comparative Survey of Socialism, Communism, Co-operation, Utopianism; and other Systems of Reform and Reconstruction. *864 pp. 16 plates. 1 figure. 1949. (3rd Impression 1960.) 50s.*

Mannheim, Karl. Freedom, Power and Democratic Planning. *Edited by Hans Gerth and Ernest K. Bramstedt. 424 pp. 1951. (2nd Impression 1965.) 35s.*

Mansur, Fatma. Process of Independence. *Foreword by A. H. Hanson. 208 pp. 1962. 25s.*

Martin, David A. Pacificism: an Historical and Sociological Study. *202 pp. 1965. 30s.*

Myrdal, Gunnar. The Political Element in the Development of Economic Theory. *Translated from the German by Paul Streeten. 282 pp. 1953. (4th Impression 1965.) 25s.*

Polanyi, Michael, F.R.S. The Logic of Liberty: Reflections and Rejoinders. *228 pp. 1951. 18s.*

Verney, Douglas V. The Analysis of Political Systems. *264 pp. 1959. (3rd Impression 1965.) 28s.*

Wootton, Graham. The Politics of Influence: British Ex-Servicemen, Cabinet Decisions and Cultural Changes, 1917 to 1957. *320 pp. 1963. 30s.*

FOREIGN AFFAIRS: THEIR SOCIAL, POLITICAL AND ECONOMIC FOUNDATIONS

Baer, Gabriel. Population and Society in the Arab East. *Translated by Hanna Szöke. 228 pp. 10 maps. 1964. 40s.*

Bonné, Alfred. The Economic Development of the Middle East: An Outline of Planned Reconstruction after the War. *192 pp. 58 tables. 1945. (3rd Impression 1953.) 16s.*

State and Economics in the Middle East: A Society in Transition. *482 pp. 2nd (revised) edition 1955. (2nd Impression 1960.) 40s.*

Studies in Economic Development: with special reference to Conditions in the Under-developed Areas of Western Asia and India. *322 pp. 84 tables. 2nd edition 1960. 32s.*

Mayer, J. P. Political Thought in France from the Revolution to the Fifth Republic. *164 pp. 3rd edition (revised) 1961. 16s.*

Schlesinger, Rudolf. Central European Democracy and its Background: Economic and Political Group Organization. *432 pp. 1953. 40s.*

Thomson, David Meyer E., and **Briggs, A.** Patterns of Peacemaking. *408 pp. 1945. 25s.*

Trouton, Ruth. Peasant Renaissance in Yugoslavia 1900-1950: A Study of the Development of Yugoslav Peasant Society as affected by Education. *370 pp. 1 map. 1952. 28s.*

CRIMINOLOGY

Ancel, Marc. Social Defence: A Modern Approach to Criminal Problems. *Foreword by Leon Radzinowicz. 240 pp. 1965. 32s.*

Cloward, Richard A., and **Ohlin, Lloyd E.** Delinquency and Opportunity: A Theory of Delinquent Gangs. *248 pp. 1961. 25s.*

Downes, David. The Delinquent Solution. A Study in Sub-cultural Theory. *304 pp. 1965. 42s.*

Dunlop, A. B., and **McCabe, S.** Young Men in Detention Centres. *192 pp. 1965. 28s.*

Friedländer, Dr. Kate. The Psycho-Analytical Approach to Juvenile Delinquency: Theory, Case Studies, Treatment. *320 pp. 1947. (5th Impression 1961.) 28s.*

Glueck, Sheldon and Eleanor. Family Environment and Delinquency. *With the statistical assistance of Rose W. Kneznek. 340 pp. 1962. 35s.*

Mannheim, Hermann. Group Problems in Crime and Punishment, and other Studies in Criminology and Criminal Law. *336 pp. 1955. 28s.*

Comparative Criminology: a Textbook. *Two volumes. 416 pp. and 360 pp. 1965. 42s. each.*

Morris, Terence. The Criminal Area: A Study in Social Ecology. *Foreword by Hermann Mannheim. 232 pp. 25 tables. 4 maps. 1957. 25s.*

5

Morris, Terence and **Pauline,** assisted by **Barbara Barer.** Pentonville: a Sociological Study of an English Prison. *416 pp. 16 plates. 1963. 50s.*

Spencer, John C. Crime and the Services. *Foreword by Hermann Mannheim. 336 pp. 1954. 28s.*

Trasler, Gordon. The Explanation of Criminality. *144 pp. 1962. 20s.*

SOCIAL PSYCHOLOGY

Barbu, Zevedei. Problems of Historical Psychology. *248 pp. 1960. 25s.*

Blackburn, Julian. Psychology and the Social Pattern. *184 pp. 1945. (7th Impression 1964.) 16s.*

Fleming, C. M. Adolescence: Its Social Psychology: With an Introduction to recent findings from the fields of Anthropology, Physiology, Medicine, Psychometrics and Sociometry. *271 pp. 2nd edition (revised) 1963. (2nd Impression 1964.) 25s.*

The Social Psychology of Education: An Introduction and Guide to Its Study. *136 pp. 2nd edition (revised) 1959. 11s.*

Fleming, C. M. (Ed.). Studies in the Social Psychology of Adolescence. *Contributions by J. E. Richardson, J. F. Forrester, J. K. Shukla and P. J. Higginbotham. Foreword by the editor. 292 pp. 29 figures. 13 tables. 5 folder tables. 1951. 23s.*

Halmos, Paul. Towards a Measure of Man: The Frontiers of Normal Adjustment. *276 pp. 1957. 28s.*

Homans, George C. The Human Group. *Foreword by Bernard DeVoto. Introduction by Robert K. Merton. 526 pp. 1951. (4th Impression 1965.) 35s.*

Social Behaviour: its Elementary Forms. *416 pp. 1961. 30s.*

Klein, Josephine. The Study of Groups. *226 pp. 31 figures. 5 tables. 1956. (4th Impression 1965.) 21s.*

Linton, Ralph. The Cultural Background of Personality. *132 pp. 1947. (5th Impression 1965.) 16s.*

Mayo, Elton. The Social Problems of an Industrial Civilization. With an appendix on the Political Problem. *180 pp. 1949. (4th Impression 1961.) 18s.*

Ridder, J. C. de. The Personality of the Urban African in South Africa. A Thematic Apperception Test Study. *196 pp. 12 plates. 1961. 25s.*

Rose, Arnold M. (Ed.). Mental Health and Mental Disorder: A Sociological Approach. *Chapters by 46 contributors. 654 pp. 1956. 45s.*

Human Behaviour and Social Processes: an Interactionist Approach. *Contributions by Arnold M. Ross, Ralph H. Turner, Anselm Strauss, Everett C. Hughes, E. Franklin Frazier, Howard S. Becker, et al. 696 pp. 1962. 60s.*

Smelser, Neil J. Theory of Collective Behaviour. *448 pp. 1962. 45s.*

Spinley, Dr. B. M. The Deprived and the Privileged: Personality Development in English Society. *232 pp. 1953. 20s.*

Wolfenstein, Martha. Disaster: A Psychological Essay. *264 pp. 1957. 23s.*

Young, Professor Kimball. Personality and Problems of Adjustment, *742 pp. 12 figures, 9 tables, 2nd edition (revised) 1952. (2nd Impression 1959.) 40s.*
Handbook of Social Psychology. *658 pp. 16 figures. 10 tables. 2nd edition (revised) 1957. (3rd Impression 1963.) 40s.*

SOCIOLOGY OF THE FAMILY

Banks, J. A. Prosperity and Parenthood: A study of Family Planning among the Victorian Middle Classes. *262 pp. 1954. (2nd Impression 1965.) 24s.*

Chapman, Dennis. The Home and Social Status. *336 pp. 8 plates. 3 figures. 117 tables. 1955. 35s.*

Klein, Josephine. Samples from English Cultures. *1965.*
  1. Three Preliminary Studies and Aspects of Adult Life in England. *447 pp. 50s.*
  2. Child-Rearing Practices and Index. *247 pp. 35s.*

Klein, Viola. Britain's Married Women Workers. *176 pp. 1965. 28s.*

Myrdal, Alva and Klein, Viola. Women's Two Roles: Home and Work. *238 pp. 27 tables. 1956. (2nd Impression 1962.) 25s.*

Parsons, Talcott and Bales, Robert F. Family: Socialization and Interaction Process. *In collaboration with James Olds, Morris Zelditch and Philip E. Slater. 456 pp. 50 figures and tables. 1956. (2nd Impression 1964.) 35s.*

THE SOCIAL SERVICES

Ashdown, Margaret and Brown, S. Clement. Social Service and Mental Health: An Essay on Psychiatric Social Workers. *280 pp. 1953. 21s.*

Hall, M. Penelope. The Social Services of Modern England. *416 pp. 6th edition (revised) 1963. (2nd Impression with a new Preface 1965.) 30s.*

Hall, M. P., and Howes, I. V. The Church in Social Work. A Study of Moral Welfare Work undertaken by the Church of England. *320 pp. 1965. 35s.*

Heywood, Jean S. Children in Care: the Development of the Service for the Deprived Child. *264 pp. 2nd edition (revised) 1965. 32s.*
An Introduction to teaching Casework Skills. *192 pp. 1964. 28s.*

Jones, Kathleen. Lunacy, Law and Conscience, 1744-1845: the Social History of the Care of the Insane. *268 pp. 1955. 25s.*
Mental Health and Social Policy, 1845-1959. *264 pp. 1960. 28s.*

Jones, Kathleen and Sidebotham, Roy. Mental Hospitals at Work. *220 pp. 1962. 30s.*

Kastell, Jean. Casework in Child Care. *Foreword by M. Brooke Willis. 320 pp. 1962. 35s.*

Rooff, Madeline. Voluntary Societies and Social Policy. *350 pp. 15 tables. 1957. 35s.*

Shenfield, B. E. Social Policies for Old Age: A Review of Social Provision for Old Age in Great Britain. *260 pp. 39 tables. 1957. 25s.*

Timms, Noel. Psychiatric Social Work in Great Britain (1939-1962). *280 pp. 1964. 32s.*

Social Casework: Principles and Practice. *256 pp. 1964, 25s.*

Trasler, Gordon. In Place of Parents: A Study in Foster Care. *272 pp. 1960. (2nd Impression 1965.) 30s.*

Young, A. F., and **Ashton, E. T.** British Social Work in the Nineteenth Century. *288 pp. 1956. (2nd Impression 1963.) 28s.*

SOCIOLOGY OF EDUCATION

Banks, Olive. Parity and Prestige in English Secondary Education: a Study in Educational Sociology. *272 pp. 1955. (2nd Impression 1963.) 28s.*

Bentwich, Joseph. Education in Israel. *224 pp. 8 pp. plates. 1965. 24s.*

Blyth, W. A. L. English Primary Education. A Sociological Description. *1965.*
1. Schools. *232 pp. 30s.*
2. Background. *168 pp. 25s.*

Collier, K. G. The Social Purposes of Education: Personal and Social Values in Education. *268 pp. 1959. (2nd Impression 1962.) 21s.*

Dale, R. R. and **Griffith, S.** Downstream: Failure in the Grammar School. *112 pp. 1965. 20s.*

Dore, R. P. Education in Tokugawa Japan. *356 pp. 9 pp. plates. 1965. 35s.*

Edmonds, E. L. The School Inspector. *Foreword by Sir William Alexander. 214 pp. 1962. 28s.*

Evans, K. M. Sociometry and Education. *158 pp. 1962. 18s.*

Foster, P. J. Education and Social Change in Ghana. *336 pp. 3 maps. 1965.*

Fraser, W. R. Education and Society in Modern France. *150 pp. 1963. 20s.*

Hans, Nicholas. New Trends in Education in the Eighteenth Century. *278 pp. 19 tables. 1951. (2nd Impression 1965.) 25s.*

Comparative Education: A Study of Educational Factors and Traditions. *360 pp. 3rd (revised) edition 1958. (4th Impression 1964.) 25s.*

Holmes, Brian. Problems in Education. A Comparative Approach. *336 pp. 1965. 32s.*

Mannheim, Karl and **Stewart, W. A. C.** An Introduction to the Sociology of Education. *208 pp. 1962. (2nd Impression 1965.) 21s.*

Musgrove, F. Youth and the Social Order. *176 pp. 1964. 21s.*

Ortega y Gasset, Jose. Mission of the University. *Translated with an Introduction by Howard Lee Nostrand. 88 pp. 1946. (3rd Impression 1963.) 15s.*

Ottaway, A. K. C. Education and Society: An Introduction to the Sociology of Education. *With an Introduction by W. O. Lester Smith. 212 pp. Second edition (revised). 1962. (3rd Impression 1965.) 21s.*

Peers, Robert. Adult Education: A Comparative Study. *398 pp. 2nd edition 1959. 35s.*

Pritchard, D. G. Education and the Handicapped: 1760 to 1960. *258 pp. 1963. 28s.*

Samuel, R. H., and **Thomas, R. Hinton.** Education and Society in Modern Germany. *212 pp. 1949. 16s.*

Simon, Brian and **Joan** (Eds.). Educational Psychology in the U.S.S.R. *Introduction by Brian and Joan Simon. Translation by Joan Simon. Papers by D. N. Bogoiavlenski and N. A. Menchinskaia, D. B. Elkonin, E. A. Fleshner, Z. I. Kalmykova, G. S. Kostiuk, V. A. Krutetski, A. N. Leontiev, A. R. Luria, E. A. Milerian, R. G. Natadze, B. M. Teplov, L. S. Vygotski, L. V. Zankov. 296 pp. 1963. 40s.*

SOCIOLOGY OF CULTURE

Fromm, Erich. The Fear of Freedom. *286 pp. 1942. (8th Impression 1960.) 21s.* The Sane Society. *400 pp. 1956. (3rd Impression 1963.) 28s.*

Mannheim, Karl. Diagnosis of Our Time: Wartime Essays of a Sociologist. *208 pp. 1943. (7th Impression 1962.) 21s.* Essays on the Sociology of Culture. *Edited by Ernst Mannheim in co-operation with Paul Kecskemeti. Editorial Note by Adolph Lowe. 280 pp. 1956. (2nd Impression 1962.) 28s.*

Weber, Alfred. Farewell to European History: or The Conquest of Nihilism. *Translated from the German by R. F. C. Hull. 224 pp. 1947. 18s.*

SOCIOLOGY OF RELIGION

Argyle, Michael. Religious Behaviour. *224 pp. 8 figures. 41 tables. 1958. (2nd Impression 1965.) 25s.*

Knight Frank H., and **Merriam, Thornton W.** The Economic Order and Religion. *242 pp. 1947. 18s.*

Watt, W. Montgomery. Islam and the Integration of Society. *320 pp. 1961. (2nd Impression.) 32s.*

SOCIOLOGY OF ART AND LITERATURE

Beljame, Alexandre. Men of Letters and the English Public in the Eighteenth Century: 1660-1744, Dryden, Addison, Pope. *Edited with an Introduction and Notes by Bonamy Dobree. Translated by E. O. Lorimer. 532 pp. 1948. 32s.*

Misch, Georg. A History of Autobiography in Antiquity. *Translated by E. W. Dickes. 2 Volumes. Vol. 1, 364 pp., Vol. 2, 372 pp. 1950. 45s. the set.*

Schucking, L. L. The Sociology of Literary Taste. *112 pp. 2nd edition, 1965. 18s.*

Silbermann, Alphons. The Sociology of Music. *224 pp. 1963. 28s.*

SOCIOLOGY OF KNOWLEDGE

Hodges, H. A. The Philosophy of Wilhelm Dilthey. *410 pp. 1952. 30s.*

Mannheim, Karl. Essays on the Sociology of Knowledge. *Edited by Paul Kecskemeti. Editorial note by Adolph Lowe. 352 pp. 1952. (3rd Impression 1964.) 35s.*

Schlesinger, Rudolf. Marx: His Time and Ours. *464 pp. 1950. (2nd Impression 1951.) 32s.*

Stark, W. America: Ideal and Reality. The United States of 1776 in Contemporary Philosophy. *136 pp. 1947. 12s.*
The Sociology of Knowledge: An Essay in Aid of a Deeper Understanding of the History of Ideas. *384 pp. 1958. (2nd Impression 1960.) 36s.*
Montesquieu: Pioneer of the Sociology of Knowledge. *244 pp. 1960. 25s.*

URBAN SOCIOLOGY

Anderson, Nels. The Urban Community: A World Perspective. *532 pp. 1960. 35s.*

Ashworth, William. The Genesis of Modern British Town Planning: A Study in Economic and Social History of the Nineteenth and Twentieth Centuries. *288 pp. 1954. (2nd Impression 1965.) 32s.*

Bracey, Howard. Neighbours: Neighbouring and Neighbourliness on New Estates and Subdivisions in England and the U.S.A. *220 pp. 1964. 28s.*

Cullingworth, J. B. Housing Needs and Planning Policy: A Restatement of the Problems of Housing Need and "Overspill" in England and Wales. *232 pp. 44 tables. 8 maps. 1960. 28s.*

Dickinson, Robert E. City and Region: A Geographical Interpretation. *608 pp. 125 figures. 1964. 60s.*
The West European City: A Geographical Interpretation. *600 pp. 129 maps. 29 plates. 2nd edition 1962. (2nd Impression 1963.) 55s.*

Dore, R. P. City Life in Japan: A Study of a Tokyo Ward. *498 pp. 8 plates. 4 figures. 24 tables. 1958. (2nd Impression 1963.) 45s.*

Jennings, Hilda. Societies in the Making: a Study of Development and Redevelopment within a County Borough. *Foreword by D. A. Clark. 286 pp. 1962. 32s.*

Kerr, Madeline. The People of Ship Street, *240 pp. 1958. 23s.*

Mann, P. H. An Approach to Urban Sociology. *240 pp. 1965. 30s.*

Morris, R. N., and **Mogey, J.** The Sociology of Housing. Studies at Berinsfield. *232 pp. 4 pp. plates. 1965. 42s.*

Rosser, C., and **Harris, C.** The Family and Social Change. A Study of Family and Kinship in a South Wales Town. *352 pp. 8 maps. 1965. 45s.*

RURAL SOCIOLOGY

Bracey, H. E. English Rural Life: Village Activities, Organizations and Institutions. *302 pp. 1959. 30s.*

Infield, Henrik F. Co-operative Living in Palestine. *With a Foreword by General Sir Arthur Wauchope, G.C.B. 170 pp. 8 plates. 7 tables. 1946. 12s. 6d.*

Littlejohn, James. Westrigg: the Sociology of a Cheviot Parish. *172 pp. 5 figures. 1963. 25s.*

Saville, John. Rural Depopulation in England and Wales, 1851-1951. *Foreword by Leonard Elmhirst. 286 pp. 6 figures. 39 tables. 1 map. 1957. 28s. (Dartington Hall Studies in Rural Sociology.)*

Williams, W. M. The Country Craftsman: A Study of Some Rural Crafts and the Rural Industries Organization in England. *248 pp. 9 figures. 1958. 25s. (Dartington Hall Studies in Rural Sociology.)*
The Sociology of an English Village: Gosforth. *272 pp. 12 figures. 13 tables. 1956. (3rd Impression 1964.) 25s.*

SOCIOLOGY OF MIGRATION

Eisenstadt, S. N. The Absorption of Immigrants: a Comparative Study based mainly on the Jewish Community in Palestine and the State of Israel. *288 pp. 1954. 28s.*

SOCIOLOGY OF INDUSTRY AND DISTRIBUTION

Anderson, Nels. Work and Leisure. *280 pp. 1961. 28s.*

Blau, Peter M., and **Scott, W. Richard.** Formal Organizations: a Comparative approach. *Introduction and Additional Bibliography by J. H. Smith. 328 pp. 1963. (2nd Impression 1964.) 28s.*

Jefferys, Margot, with the assistance of Winifred Moss. Mobility in the Labour Market: Employment Changes in Battersea and Dagenham. *Preface by Barbara Wootton. 186 pp. 51 tables. 1954. 15s.*

Levy, A. B. Private Corporations and Their Control. *Two Volumes. Vol. 1, 464 pp., Vol. 2, 432 pp. 1950. 80s. the set.*

Levy, Hermann. The Shops of Britain: A Study of Retail Distribution. *268 pp. 1948. (2nd Impression 1949.) 21s.*

Liepmann, Kate. The Journey to Work: Its Significance for Industrial and Community Life. *With a Foreword by A. M. Carr-Saunders. 230 pp. 40 tables. 3 folders. 1944. (2nd Impression 1945.) 18s.*
Apprenticeship: An Enquiry into its Adequacy under Modern Conditions. *Foreword by H. D. Dickinson. 232 pp. 6 tables. 1960. (2nd Impression.) 23s.*

Millerson, Geoffrey. The Qualifying Associations: a Study in Professionalization. *320 pp. 1964. 42s.*

Smelser, Neil J. Social Change in the Industrial Revolution: An Application of Theory to the Lancashire Cotton Industry, 1770-1840. *468 pp. 12 figures. 14 tables. 1959. (2nd Impression 1960.) 40s.*

Williams, Gertrude. Recruitment to Skilled Trades. *240 pp. 1957. 23s.*

Young, A. F. Industrial Injuries Insurance: an Examination of British Policy. *192 pp. 1964. 30s.*

ANTHROPOLOGY
(*Demy 8vo.*)

Crook, David and **Isabel**. Revolution in a Chinese Village: Ten Mile Inn. *230 pp. 8 plates. 1 map. 1959. 21s.*

The First Years of Yangyi Commune. *288 pp. 12 plates. 1965. 42s.*

Dube, S. C. Indian Village. *Foreword by Morris Edward Opler. 276 pp. 4 plates. 1955. (5th Impression 1965.) 25s.*

India's Changing Villages: Human Factors in Community Development *260 pp. 8 plates. 1 map. 1958. (2nd Impression 1960.) 25s.*

Fei, Hsiao-Tung. Peasant Life in China: a Field Study of Country Life in the Yangtze Valley. *Foreword by Bronislaw Malinowski. 320 pp. 14 plates. 1939. (5th Impression 1962.) 30s.*

Firth, Raymond. Malay Fishermen. Their Peasant Economy. *420 pp. 17 pp. plates. 2nd edition (revised and enlarged 1965.) 55s.*

Gulliver, P. H. The Family Herds. A Study of two Pastoral Tribes in East Africa, The Jie and Turkana. *304 pp. 4 plates. 19 figures. 1955. 25s.*

Social Control in an African Society: a Study of the Arusha, Agricultural Masai of Northern Tanganyika. *320 pp. 8 plates. 10 figures. 1963. 35s.*

Hogbin, Ian. Transformation Scene. The Changing Culture of a New Guinea Village. *340 pp. 22 plates. 2 maps. 1951. 30s.*

Hsu, Francis L. K. Under the Ancestors' Shadow: Chinese Culture and Personality. *346 pp. 26 figures. 1949. 21s.*

Lowie, Professor Robert H. Social Organization. *494 pp. 1950. (3rd Impression 1962.) 35s.*

Maunier, René. The Sociology of Colonies: An Introduction to the Study of Race Contact. *Edited and translated by E. O. Lorimer. 2 Volumes. Vol. 1, 430 pp. Vol. 2, 356 pp. 1949. 70s. the set.*

Mayer, Adrian C. Caste and Kinship in Central India: A Village and its Region, *328 pp. 16 plates. 15 figures. 16 tables. 1960. (2nd Impression 1965.) 35s.*

Peasants in the Pacific: A Study of Fiji Indian Rural Society. *232 pp. 16 plates. 10 figures. 14 tables. 1961. 35s.*

Osborne, Harold. Indians of the Andes: Aymaras and Quechuas. *292 pp. 8 plates. 2 maps. 1952. 25s.*

Smith, Raymond T. The Negro Family in British Guiana: Family Structure and Social Status in the Villages. *With a Foreword by Meyer Fortes. 314 pp. 8 plates. 1 figure. 4 maps. 1956. (2nd Impression 1965.) 28s.*

DOCUMENTARY
(Demy 8vo.)

Meek, Dorothea L. (Ed.). Soviet Youth: Some Achievements and Problems. *Excerpts from the Soviet Press, translated by the editor. 280 pp. 1957. 28s.*

Schlesinger, Rudolf (Ed.). Changing Attitudes in Soviet Russia.

1. The Family in the U.S.S.R. *Documents and Readings, with an Introduction by the editor. 434 pp. 1949. 30s.*

2. The Nationalities Problem and Soviet Administration. Selected Readings on the Development of Soviet Nationalities Policies. *Introduced by the editor. Translated by W. W. Gottlieb. 324 pp. 1956. 30s.*

Reports
of the Institute
# of Community Studies

(Demy 8vo.)

Cartwright, Ann. Human Relations and Hospital Care. *272 pp. 1964. 30s.*

Jackson, Brian. Streaming: an Education System in Miniature. *168 pp. 1964. 21s. Paper 10s.*

Jackson, Brian and **Marsden, Dennis.** Education and the Working Class: Some General Themes raised by a Study of 88 Working-class Children in a Northern Industrial City. *268 pp. 2 folders. 1962. (3rd Impression 1965.) 28s.*

Marris, Peter. Widows and their Families. *Foreword by Dr. John Bowlby. 184 pp. 18 tables. Statistical Summary. 1958. 18s.*
Family and Social Change in an African City. A Study of Rehousing in Lagos. *196 pp. 1 map. 4 plates. 53 tables. 1961. 25s.*
The Experience of Higher Education. *232 pp. 27 tables. 1964. 25s.*

Mills, Enid. Living with Mental Illness: a Study in East London. *Foreword by Morris Carstairs. 196 pp. 1962. 28s.*

Runciman, W. G. Relative Deprivation and Social Justice. *344 pp. 1966. 40s.*

Townsend, Peter. The Family Life of Old People: An Inquiry in East London. *Foreword by J. H. Sheldon. 300 pp. 3 figures. 63 tables. 1957. (2nd Impression 1961.) 30s.*

Willmott, Peter. The Evolution of a Community: a study of Dagenham after forty years. *168 pp. 2 maps. 1963. 21s.*

Willmott, Peter and **Young, Michael.** Family and Class in a London Suburb. *202 pp. 47 tables. 1960. (2nd Impression 1961.) 21s.*

Young, Michael. Innovation and Research in Education. *192 pp. 1965. 25s.*

Young, Michael and **Willmott, Peter.** Family and Kinship in East London. *Foreword by Richard M. Titmuss. 252 pp. 39 tables. 1957. (3rd Impression 1965.) 25s.*

The British Journal of Sociology. *Edited by Terence P. Morris. Vol. 1, No. 1, March 1950 and Quarterly. Roy 8vo., £2 10s. p.a.; 12s. 6d. a number, post free.*

All prices are net and subject to alteration without notice